JEFFREY W. AUBUCHON

Flight School

Lessons with Peter Pan

92252 PRESS

First published by 92252 Press 2020

First edition

ISBN: 978-1-7340592-3-6

Cover art by Anna Burrous

This book was professionally typeset on Reedsy.
Find out more at reedsy.com

To Kris DeMoura,
the Oakmont music teacher who reminds me every day I can fly.

&

To the students who welcomed Peter Pan to our school in 2018:
AA, AD, AG, AL, AL, AM, AM, AP, AP, AR, AV, AV, AW, CC, CD, CE, CK, CS, DB, EB, EG, EK, EP, EP, ER, ET, EW, GD, HF, HG, IG, JB, JC, JK, JM, JP, KA, KM, KR, LB, LMC, LD, MA, MB, MB, MC, MC, ML, MM, MS, MV, OD, OS, OW, PB, RM, SA, SK, SM, SR, SR, SV, T & CR, TMC, TP, VL & WB

Mr. DeMoura and I believe you can fly past the stars—each of you!

In 1929, J. M. Barrie bequeathed *Peter Pan* to Great Ormond Street Hospital for Children in London, which has benefited thousands of children ever since.

A portion of each theatre ticket sold to a performance of *Peter Pan*, as well as $1 from every copy of *Flight School*, helps to make the stellar hospital the bright center of hope it is today.

Visit donate.gosh.org to help even more children fly, because, as Sir James noticed, ***all children, except one, grow up.***

Contents

III Part Three

IV The End

Foreword

One of the richest experiences in life is to be a part of a vibrant community with all its strengths and joys. Jeffrey Aubuchon in his book *Flight School* explores how developing community is a process that can bring joy, but frustration as well. Ultimately, however, the process is what makes a community vibrant and desirable.

Community is revealed in many different forms in *Flight School*. We see the community of two small towns in central Massachusetts, which form a regional school district. We see the community within a regional high school and the world of teens and adults there. We see the community of the theatre program, which ambitiously staged the musical *Peter Pan* with all its technical and social challenges. As Aubuchon skillfully looks at each of these specific communities, he presents a larger and universal view of community building and how it happens.

Foremost a teacher, Aubuchon views theatre as another avenue for instilling learning and understanding. In his role as theatre director at Oakmont Regional High School in the towns of Ashburnham and Westminter, Massachusetts, he chose plays that would interest students and the community, but also stretch them in new directions. In choosing *Peter Pan*, he knew that there would be challenges, after all, characters fly! But there was also the challenge of reimagining an older play with stereotypical views of Native Americans. He needed to work effectively with a local Native American group to help students understand the stereotypes and present the characters in a more sensitive manner.

Flight School takes us along with Aubuchon as he builds community within his theatre group, the school, the towns, and the world beyond to stage a production that engaged students and challenged stereotypes. He does not sugar-coat the process. He honestly shows the ups and downs and hard work it takes to put on a production and work collaboratively with teenagers and adults. After all, teens (and adults!) have their own ideas about schedules and ways of doing things. Through narrative, emails, texts, and interviews, he outlines the process with all its nail-biting tension and exquisite joy. Ultimately, Aubuchon shows that a community can bring a sense of accomplishment and closeness that cannot be found in a "do-it-yourself" world. *Flight School* is not just a theatre director's story of putting on a stage production. It is a larger picture of people working together to better themselves and society and find new ways of looking at the world.

Diane K. Erickson, Ed.D.
Chair (ret.), Dept. of English Language Arts
Oakmont Regional High School

From West Yarmouth on Cape Cod, January, 2020

Author's Note

When I graduated from library school and worked as a librarian, I often thought about categorizing books on a shelf. I've similarly thought about where to put this book: it's a story, and a memoir, and a travelogue, and it's creative nonfiction; it gives some lessons to high school directors and parents—less about directing *Peter Pan* and more about fostering an inclusive program—and even studies some storybook characters. Read it if you feel ageless like Peter Pan. Or read it to appreciate life in a rural American high school in 2018. The story tells of an eighteen-month journey directing, organizing, and raising money to help kids fly just like *Peter Pan.* If you've not read the 1911 novel by J.M. Barrie, read the companion *Peter and Wendy,* also from 92252 Press, on this journey.

In telling this story, I've spent as much time crafting words as publishing them. In this digital age where email and text messages document so much, I've reprinted some conversations and also reconstructed some from memory and follow-up questions. Like Frank McCourt in *Angela's Ashes* and Roddy Doyle in *Paddy Clarke Ha Ha Ha*, I've omitted quotations marks from the dialog; instead, I've italicized those recreated discussions and written remarks remain offset by quotation marks. A bibliographic essay explains the sources I consulted. While the narrative draws together numerous voices from the community, the book focuses on two stories beyond my own—those of music teacher Kris DeMoura and engineering teacher Dave Lantry. All of Oakmont owes so much to Kris and Dave for their limitless gifts to the school. My friend, the songwriter John Flanagan, also makes a brief appearance in the story. I remain grateful to a retired Oakmont teacher, Dr. Diane Erickson, for introducing the book.

Original design by Steph Seifert for the cast t-shirt

I

Part One

In the first act, we exchange the routine of our world
for the innocence of the Darling nursery,
only to have it disrupted by a boy—
a boy who refused to grow up.

Overture

My sister and I walked arm-in-arm along the south bank of the Thames, not far from the London Eye, on a chilly Saturday night in December of 2016. Despite the seventeen-year gap in our ages, we have learned that we travel quite well together—especially on this, Jenn's first trip to London. We inherited our blue eyes from our father, along with his sense of humor. She, however, got Mom's wavy brown hair, which she keeps below her shoulders, while mine greys at an Olympic speed like Dad's. We're also great friends. *The Palace of Westminster,* I said pointing to Parliament, again playing the history teacher. *Westminster. Like the town back home.*

She nodded silently, choosing to appease, rather than insult.

Did you see him? I asked, trying to break the awkward pause.

What?

Peter Pan. Did you see him? There, I pointed at the tower, *he flew across the clock face.*

Ha, she said, letting her breath escape. I saw a small grin.

As we continued to walk, I kept my eyes to the dark rooflines and chimney stacks I knew both from film and my travels as I thought more of Peter Pan. Even over dinner and mulled wine, despite talking about Christmas and our plans for the next day, I focused on Peter Pan. I hadn't watched a movie about him since childhood, although I read the 1911 novel one summer in my twenties. Later, I checked the window latch when I turned out the lights and drew the curtains across the tall windows of the Edwardian house where we slept. Even with the latch fastened, Peter Pan visited me in my sleep that night.

After a full English breakfast the next morning, we headed toward Victoria Station to catch a train to Canterbury. Sunlight replaced the darkness, but the December chill kept our breath visible. I stopped in a corridor formed by white London townhouses, turned to Jenn and said: *We're going to stage Peter Pan next year.*

What? she asked, sounding just as she had the night before.

Next year, at Oakmont, for the musical. We're going to put Peter Pan on stage.

Doesn't he fly? Like, off the stage? We're talking Oakmont.

I know. Yes, he does—well, she—a girl usually plays Peter.

This is only your second year directing again, isn't Grease enough for Oakmont?

Can't you see him—er, her? Flying? Right off the stage? Not just Peter, but Wendy and the boys, too?

We walked on and she remained pensive for a few steps; Jenn seemed to be thinking with her hands in her pockets. She had only just graduated from Oakmont in June, but it was as much her school as mine, first when I grew up there as a student and later as a teacher.

It's brilliant, she said. *So long as I get a flight. And my pet goats can have a small part.*

Ha. I laughed, *maybe a flight, but there are no goats in the story,* I said, taking her arm like the Scarecrow did for Dorothy, and we set off to catch our train to Kent.

Act I, Scene 1: Kris

Are you crazy? Kris asked, looking up from his office desk at 6:20 am on Monday as I handed him a venti cold brew coffee with sweet cream from Starbucks. *You fly to London for the weekend, which is crazy enough, and come back thinking you're going to fly kids with a rope? Thanks for the Starbucks, by the way.* Kris DeMoura has directed the Oakmont Regional High School music program since 2000, not only garnering great respect in the towns of Ashburnham and Westminster that comprise the school district but across Massachusetts. On his desk sit many awards, including two for his music direction of Oakmont's *Into the Woods* and *Les Misérables.* Kris and I had worked well together since my return to Oakmont, but starting in 2016 when the principal appointed me director of the musical, we became inseparable. While I had overall responsibility for the production, Kris taught the music and conducted the professional orchestra.

In addition to the numerous awards for his ensembles, Disney memorabilia clutter Kris's windowless office. Parading the Marching Spartans down Main Street, U.S.A. at Walt Disney World every three years serves as the highlight of his work. I have loved watching Kris—even more than the students—when he walks with his seventy-strong marching band through the park. Sure, I'm proud of the kids, too, but seeing Kris radiate makes the trip entirely worthwhile and it's an event I've not missed since 2012. There has also been a big transformation in Kris from 2015 to 2018. We rode the Thunder Mountain Railroad in 2015 with great hilarity, but I didn't bounce around the cart much. In 2018, we rode the rollercoaster again, but this time I couldn't stay put as the train twisted and turned: Kris had lost much weight in the intervening years, making his friends and family both proud of, and happy for, him. I'm at least four inches taller than he, and now he's twenty-five pounds lighter than I am. While he never tires of teasing my white hair—even more now that it's dyed—I'm quick to remind him of his baldness. He usually sports a beard and almost always dresses in a necktie at school, and he's much more dedicated to the tie than I am. My pale skin contrasts with his Portuguese tones (his father emigrated from the Azores) and, while I always wear glasses, I only recently learned he wears contact lenses. Although no one would confuse us for biological brothers, there are few people, if any besides my sister, I trust more than Kris.

Yes, you know I'm crazy, but can't you see it? Can't you imagine the kids flying?

He thought for a moment, sat back in his chair, smiled like Jenn, and said, *Yes. But isn't that little kid stuff? Is that the kind of show you want to do for a high school?*

It's timeless. It's about friendship. And never growing up. And believing to fly. What's typical, Kris?

Oklahoma!, Kiss Me Kate, or even Grease like we're doing in April.[1] He paused. *The flying sounds cool, but you better ask Mr. Uminski before you get too far into this stuff.*

Do you like it?

I'm warming to it; it's only 6:30 in the morning. We'll make it work for us.

It'll be great. I can see it.

I couldn't get to the principal's office until B Block (9:30 am). I told him the idea, just as I had Kris, and typical of Mr. Uminski, he answered with perfunctory enthusiasm: *Perfect. I love it.*

Do you understand it involves flying, Mr. U?

It's got to be safe, no? We're not the first to do it. It's perfect, he said swiveling back to his computer to deal with the challenges that face a high school principal. I had Mr. Uminski as a teacher for Western Civilization in the tenth grade and years later in 2011, when a member of faculty became terminally ill, he reached me via my mother to ask if I would return to teach with almost immediate effect. I did, and Oakmont once again became my life. *Let me know what you find out about the insurance*, he said, pecking at his keyboard as I turned to leave.

Let's keep it a secret until everything is in place, I said.

Perfect. He nodded as he continued to peck.

I detoured into the auditorium on my return to my classroom. Just two weeks earlier we closed the fall production—the annual weekend of one-act plays called the Interclass Festival—and the post-production stage looked unusually clean. I sat for a moment in my favorite seat, J9, and stared at the dauntingly-high proscenium. *They'll fly,* I thought. *We all will.*

When I graduated from Oakmont in 1998, the nearly forty-year-year-old building confessed its age. Five years later, the towns funded a major renovation with a beautiful addition to the front of the building. During school hours, workers transformed the old, windowless, cave-like library into classrooms with skylights. A vaulted open space with soaring ceilings now greeted visitors at the front of the building as a temple to books. The redesigned art studios displayed student artwork in a wall of windows overlooking the lobby. The builders added a new gym to the rear of the building, behind what we now call "the old gym," where I had sweat and even square danced as a teen. The designers also banished the orange fabrics of the auditorium curtains—ever an enigma for a school with green and white colors—and in their place, they transformed a space that celebrates the performing arts with light-colored woods that brighten the dark space with its 481 seats. Although not a pretentious stage, Alumni Auditorium serves as a home for the rural school's award-winning music ensembles and theatre troupe, and a space to celebrate academic achievement.

The rest of the school also received a much-needed cleaning during the renovation. New science laboratories and a greenhouse adjoined the downstairs wing—the greenhouse positioned just behind the end zone of the football field with protective nets—while the gutted band room stayed in place with its high ceilings. The architects expanded an intersection called "Four Corners," the area with the greatest student traffic flow, to include a skylight to allow for natural light. Many, if not all, students pass through and congregate in Four Corners every day, serving as the hub of learning with the English and language arts classrooms reaching towards the north, the social studies and music departments to the south, the engineering shops, auditorium, and art studios to the east, and math and sciences downstairs. The towns of Ashburnham and Westminster have cared for Oakmont since its opening day in 1960, but even now, the walls need paint and some ceiling tiles need to be replaced. Maintenance never ends for Mike

Parenteau, the school's chief custodian, and his dedicated crew, but generally, both students and staff show their appreciation and care for the space. Mike stands tall as a burly dad in his fifties and a proud alumnus of the Oakmont football team. For all the tasks asked of him, he only ever says, "roger that" and he and his crew work hard to make Oakmont a clean and safe space in which students and teachers both learn and grow. I'm not sure that happens in all schools, but it does at Oakmont.

The story of Ashburnham and Westminster mimics Dickens' tale of two cities. Quaint village centers, abundant forests with lakes, as well as suburban housing developments—modest in Ashburnham and more substantial in Westminster—comprise both towns. Ashburnham, where I grew up, lies to the north on the border of New Hampshire with a population of 6,304 and a median household income of $81,324. Almost no industry remains in the town and only a handful of shops have stayed on Main Street. A serious grocer must travel twenty minutes to either Gardner or Fitchburg to do a full shop. To the south, more affluent Westminster enjoys the benefit of laying along the Massachusetts Route 2 corridor, providing commuters easy access to Boston and jobs within the "128 Belt," with a population of 7,277 and slightly higher household income at $83,597. The median household income for all of Massachusetts sits at $77,385, placing both towns above average.[2] Westminster benefits from more industry and, while the town keeps "big box" stores out, access to Route 2 makes shopping much more convenient for Westminster residents than those of Ashburnham. These towns generally represent an ethnically homogeneous part of Massachusetts. Lack of public transportation and the inability to easily get around either town, coupled with a lack of affordable rental housing, have not attracted immigrant families like the nearby cities of Gardner and Fitchburg.[3] Among the four schools in the towns: two elementary, a middle school, and the high school, the district employs only one full-time teacher for English Language Learners; however, enough diversity exists to fund the position and the "face" of the schools thankfully no longer looks as homogeneous as in my youth.

Ashburnham and Westminster residents rightly boast of their football, field hockey, basketball, and baseball teams—among others. They appreciate the students' high achievement on state and national tests and applaud the continued excellence of the music program whose members annually receive gold and platinum state recognition. The annual Evening With the Arts showcases students' brilliance not only in the visual arts but also in a mind-blowing array of engineering inventions, video game design, and robots. For a school of around 700 students, these students achieve much in rural Massachusetts every year.

The theatre program at Oakmont, however, has ebbed and flowed in its popularity since 1960. For thirty-five years, Mr. John Blackwell—my music teacher and director—produced a biannual Rodgers and Hammerstein-type musical as part of the music program. Following his retirement in 2000, the program entered a period of reorganization before Mrs. Sandy Couture began her service in 2005 as an after-school director and added other perennial favorites like *Guys & Dolls*, *Kiss Me Kate*, and *Anything Goes* to the program's repertoire.[4] This excellence continued under Emily Smith who worked with Sandy and brought a new generation of shows starting in 2010, notably *Urinetown*, *Young Frankenstein*, and *Seussical,* to Oakmont. Both Sandy and Emily, as external directors, had to engage with students and faculty after the school day. When Emily adjusted her career beyond Oakmont, I wanted to take the reins of the program, and I knew my approach differed from the previous three directors. Mr. Blackwell focused on choral singing, but I relied on Kris to help with that. Sandy and Emily brought serious technical expertise to the stage, especially with set building and, although I'm the son and grandson of carpenters, I can't bang nails. I worked to build community through Oakmont Theatre by finding a place for everyone on the stage, amplifying the unique voice of every student participant, innovating for the program with new things like flying, and giving wider and more inclusive audiences an enjoyable experience with familiar stories. In 2017, the two towns demonstrated this unity with their love of *Grease*. By the time the curtain rose that April, town residents had bought all the 1,443 tickets to all three performances.

Preparations for the *Grease* season began long before April; indeed, Kris and I, with Karen Brown our choreographer, held auditions the week before Christmas vacation. Students in the program represented a range of theatre experiences. For example, Maura, who played Sandy, later gained admittance to the highly-competitive musical theatre program at Emerson College while some of the fifty-five cast members stood on stage for the very first time. With help from Kris, I found an amazing, full-sized Greased Lightnin' for the boys to wheel on stage, and Karen not only gave the kids jivin' dance moves, but she also gave them the confidence to step, flip, and kick. The team's efforts paid off with standing ovations at every performance. The journey from a traditional Rodgers & Hammerstein production of *The Sound of Music* the year before to Rockin' Rydell High in 2017 gave Oakmont Theatre a new direction. *We all have to grow*, my good friend and engineering teacher Dave Lantry said. *You can't do The Sound of Music every year.*

As I joined the kids on stage when they took their final bows at the Saturday, April 8, 2017 evening performance of *Grease*, I thanked them, their parents, and the many staff members who made the event possible. With a nod to Karen, who doubled as stage manager, she produced a 24" x 24" box from stage left, which I held for Maura, the club president, as I said to the audience: *when she pulls out the treasure, you'll know next year's show.* A drum roll came from the pit as Maura shakily opened the package. She looked at me first, smiled, and in a style fitting for someone pursuing a life on the stage, pulled out the great Captain's hook to the shrieks and applause of the audience. *Come see them fly next April!* I said and waved the *Grease* audience goodbye as the orchestra played *We Go Together* a final time. *Peter Pan* no longer turned in my mind as a fantasy—indeed, I had mailed the signed contract the day before—we would fly to Neverland in 2018. As I walked backstage with the kids, I looked up into the bright stage lights and rafters behind the proscenium. *Thirty feet is awfully high*, I thought before turning to help sort the costumes and put Greased Lightnin' in the garage. *Thirty feet. It might as well be the stars.*

The thing about Peter Pan, I thought lying in bed at 6:30 the morning after *Grease* closed, *it's all about kids. Little kids.* My mind turned. *How can we get kids to the show?* By 9:00 I had a plan, and it seemed a perfectly respectable time to text Kris.

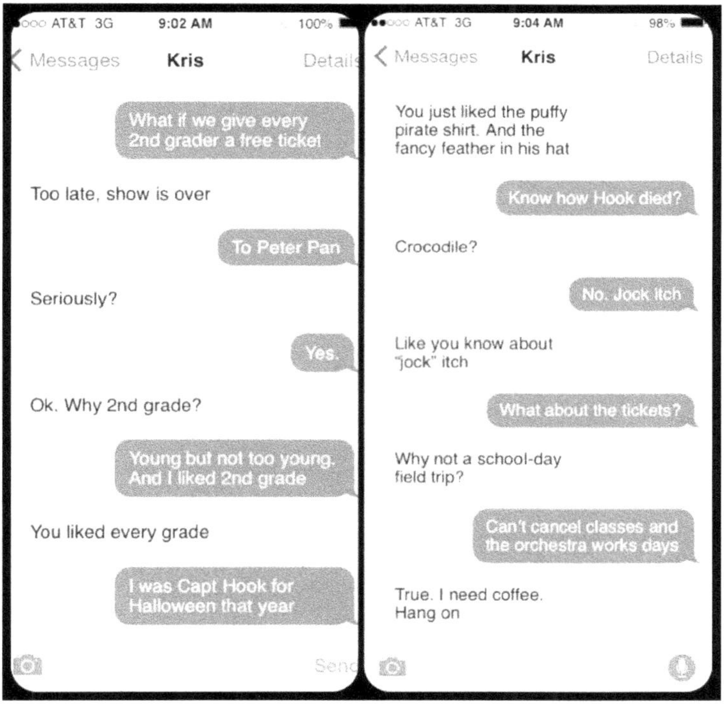

We paused to brew coffee. *What's the goal?* I mused aloud to Mr. Keurig. *Get kids in seats. Not just kids, but families. Without barrier. We've got to open the doors to everyone.* I resumed my texting:

When I asked the students in the fall of 2015 what we should tackle for our first production together, they emphatically wanted a traditional Rodgers & Hammerstein show. In recent memory, Oakmont had successfully produced some rather contemporary musicals and *The Sound of Music* represented a departure from these. The towns appreciated the students' choice. *Isn't it a lovely story?* I often heard. One woman said: *this is the third, maybe fourth time I've seen The Sound of Music at Oakmont, I just love it here.* A grandfather told me: *I saw it advertised in the newspaper. I live in Fitchburg and I brought my friend because the music is so beautiful.* I gleaned a few lessons from staging *The Sound of Music* that *Peter Pan* helped bring into greater focus for me, and both Kris and engineering teacher Dave Lantry helped me understand these:

First, there's no replacing a good story. Residents of Ashburnham and Westminster want to see a good, and familiar, story. If the story is good, and the kids perform well, a few added surprises make the audience happy. Our community doesn't generally expect Broadway; rather, they want a wholesome night to see their kids, and their neighbors' kids, smiling on stage. As Kris says, *we need to make the show our own.*

Second, as Dave Lantry said, *you can't do The Sound of Music every year. You've got to grow.* Despite being the real boy who never wanted to grow up, Dave, like all of us, has made his life work to help kids grow. So each year, I chose a show in consultation with Kris that pushed us to grow in a new way. Of course, we would grow in many different ways, but each season we focused on one way in particular. With *Peter Pan*, I imagined we would grow with flying and new effects, but we grew further as we included more and more guests in the production.

Finally, just like the Lost Boys (and Girls),[5] everyone wants to be asked to play a "role" in the play. Not everyone in town comes to the show, but many students, teachers, and residents want to be invited—even if only to decline. Outreach and inclusion—not simply advertising—fosters community spirit. While this book explores all three of these lessons, *Peter Pan* taught me, and perhaps the whole community taught me, mostly about the importance of inclusion.

In the spirit of growing, then, we moved from *The Sound of Music* to the more up-tempo *Grease.* The goal for growing included welcoming more boys in the cast and learning a different kind of performance style than we used in 2016. As the director, I also worked hard behind the scenes of *Grease* to streamline the finances and incorporate some fun things in the production like cast t-shirts. Where the prior directors would build original sets, I preferred to use rented backdrops because Oakmont has very little room for construction and storage. I found the right pieces to assemble a vintage set: high-top diner tables with classic red diner stools, simple car silhouettes for the drive-in with colored LED lights installed by the engineering students, and Greased Lightnin' with working headlights. Schools with bigger budgets could surely produce showier stuff. If you're looking for a story about fireworks and stars on the flight to Neverland, this isn't the book for you. At Oakmont, I managed a tick-tight budget, and as the master director William Ball noted, the lack of money is "one of the limitations that causes creativity" (159). This book chronicles our journey, in a small rural high school, when sometimes we reached the stars, sometimes we surpassed them, and sometimes—more often than I would have liked—we fell short. Kris and I strove to maintain the energy this book tries to capture each year we collaborated—not measured by sold-out seats, and never universally successful, but with an enthusiastic sense of belonging that's impossible to quantify. It's the same sense Kris so expertly imbues in his award-winning Marching Spartans band in Walt Disney World. Staging *Peter Pan*, just like our other adventures, became our most imperfect flight to Neverland.

Act I, Scene 2: John

As our engines revved for *Grease*, I reconnected with an old friend. John Flanagan and I had met years before and our friendship has often shifted like the tide; friends always but with varying intensity. Other than my family, only John knew me during my marriage, or when my daughter Arabella died, or saw me through my divorce. We shared happy times, too, and John always seemed to be present as I passed important milestones in my life. *Come to California for spring break and tell me all about Grease*, he had said on the phone. I hadn't been to California in a few years and, while I wouldn't crash on John's couch, it would be good to visit him and get away. I splurged, relishing the success of *Grease*, booked an ocean-view room at Laguna Beach and rented a sporty car to drive the coast. *I've got a gig Thursday night, meet me there in Beverly Hills,* he said. *It's not far from Sunset Boulevard.*

I packed light—just a knapsack—with shorts, tees, flip-flops, and something just slightly dressy for Thursday night. I brought along my old, well-worn 1911 original copy of *Peter and Wendy*, which I had unearthed when I returned from London. I thumbed through it when I needed inspiration for the show and I figured I'd read a bit of it on the plane. John gave me that copy when I returned from Peace Corps service in Morocco, after a period when we had lost contact. The book served as sort of a peace offering then and, while we were far from war in 2017, things still felt a little distant. I hoped the book would ease my nerves about seeing him again. In my anxiety, I texted Kris from my hotel room.

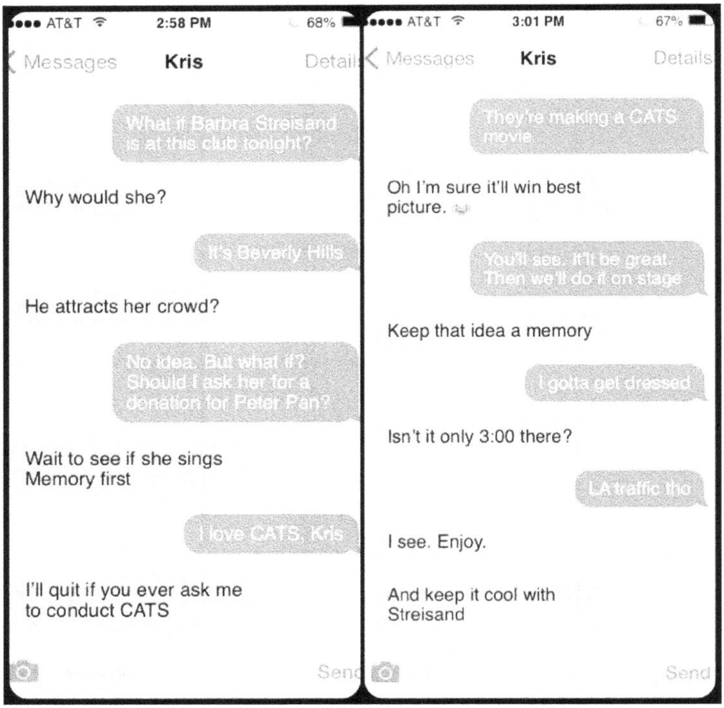

I first heard John sing with his new band *Faultlines* that night. He formed his band with two friends from their previous performance work at Disneyland. John wrote most of the original folk revival music, but they also sang covers at restaurant gigs like this. He waved as I walked in and sat down at the back of the patio. He threw in a bit of Cher during that set (which he dedicated to *someone who had traveled a long way to hear it*) and came right over to my table at the first break. We hugged. The kind of hug you get from a sibling. I'm sure he's hoping as he reads this that I describe him as an eternally-youthful Peter Pan. I'm not. At 32 he's the same age as my brother but admittedly looks better than I did then with my prematurely-grey hair. Unlike Peter Pan, however, John is certainly growing up. Like Kris, his skin tans far more easily than mine—I only burn—in the California sun. If you described me as serious, it would be hard to describe John as anything but fun. His eyes, however, are arresting. Not their brown color, but there's something about how he squints when he laughs that puts you instantly at ease.

How's your family? I asked.

Same. Yours?

Same.

How old is Jenn?

Graduated.

No way. All grown up? How's Oakmont without her?

Same as it was fifteen years ago when I was there. We laughed.

He asked about *Grease* and I told him of *Peter Pan.*

Woof, he said. *Flying. That's Disney stuff.*

I suppose. Are you still performing at Disneyland?

Ya, but as a contractor, not an employee. We sing Faultlines songs instead of Disney songs. It's good.

I see. The park seems to have been a good start for you in L.A.

It has, and now we can branch out with our own band.

It's great, John. I'm really proud of you. I watched him look at the time on his phone. *Got time for lunch tomorrow before I fly out?*

Absolutely.

Where?

Let's say Zinc Café. In the Arts District. You'll love it.

See you at noon, then.

I ate through a few more sets and John came to visit in between. The conversation remained shallow with things like: *You're on Twitter? Hilarious. How did I not know this? I'll follow you.* I slipped out just before the end to avoid a prolonged goodbye, but the last thing he said to me stuck: *Peter Pan sounds great. Your excitement makes you look happy again. I know it's been a rough couple of years since the divorce, but I'm glad to see a bit of your joy return.* I thought about his words as I drove south along the I-5 in the dark and I relaxed as the Pacific breeze hit my face through the open window. I climbed into bed in my seaside hotel with the old copy of *Peter and Wendy* sleeping on the nightstand. I didn't open it, I just remember it quietly kept me company.

I came to understand the horrors of Los Angeles traffic while staying south of the city. I proved far too "east coast" in my attempted punctuality. Zinc Café, like much of the L.A. Arts District, appears as a converted industrial space with cement floors, rustic tables, a comfortable courtyard, and a generous bar protesting the swankier places in town—places where John performed. The lunch conversation resumed easier than it had unfolded the night before.

It's been good to see you, John.

You, too. What will you do with all your post-Grease free time?

Eh. Finish the school year, teach summer school, and probably start to tackle Peter Pan.

I'm surprised it's not CATS.

I have resistance, I laughed. *No, Peter Pan will be just great.*

Have you ever watched "Peter Pan Gone Wrong" on YouTube?

It's hilarious.

Don't even mention an accident. I'm serious.

Ok, ok, he laughed again. *How about you rest this summer, Jeff?*

Not likely.

I thought your part of Massachusetts was lovely in summer. You used to love hiking, enjoy vacation!

Well, I teach in the country but I don't quite live there. My city is hardly idyllic.

It's not far though.

You traded New England for California.

Yes, I did. He grinned. *So who's going to be Peter?*

No idea. That's what auditions are for.

Do you have talent?

Yeah, we do—largely because the kids' musical skills are so good thanks to Kris.

Who's Kris?

The music teacher. Great friend. A couple of kids are really serious about community theatre, too.

It must be a joy—they must be so excited to be on stage. His eyes widened.

Mostly.

Mostly?

I'm not sure I reach them all.

How so?

Of course you do, you just need to be patient so the seeds grow.

I'm sure.

Here. Happy birthday. Early. He slid a CD in a white cardboard sleeve across the table.

Your album?

Ya.

Thank you. And you're a whole month early, I said.

None of the covers we sang last night. All original stuff I wrote.

Thanks, John, I looked up. *I'll play it as I head to the airport. I should go though.*

We stood and hugged and took a goofy selfie, but made no plans to visit each other in the future.

Keep me up-to-date about Neverland, ok? he said as we parted. *And don't watch 'Peter Pan Gone Wrong' too many times.*

K. See you soon-ish, Friend.

Apart from my initial conversations with John and Kris, who were only critical out of true curiosity, I never had to justify staging *Peter Pan* to anyone in town—and it surprised me. Not all of my choices for a show are greeted so enthusiastically, but our community embraced *Peter Pan*—even though it's more than a century old and with countless film adaptations. Is the story timeless? Sure. Did the flying excite our little towns? Maybe. Many people said, *I know about Peter Pan, but I don't know the story.* Yet, I never encountered any resistance to *Peter Pan* from any segment within the community—many, it seemed to me, extended their hand to welcome Peter Pan as a friend.

Most of us remember the catchphrases from *Peter Pan*, about never growing up and the second star to the left. Those, like me, who grew up after the Disney and Broadway productions of the 1950s recall Peter's elvish daring, Wendy's care for the others, the sense of belonging for which the Lost Boys (and Girls) yearn, and the innocence of young Michael and his bear. Adults often appreciate both Mrs. Darling's motherly protection and Mr. Darling's financial woes. Often, although not in our production, Mr. Darling doubles as Captain Hook, blending the boundary between what children see and imagine.

Hook represents the most complex of Barrie's characters, as both a caricature of the old aristocracy that kneeled to the industrial world of Mr. Darling, but also a sad creature whom we pity in his loneliness. Bravery, maternalism, and most importantly friendship permeate *Peter Pan* and call to us from a century later. Although Barrie wrote the play for the English stage, Disney Americanized it in the 1950s and preserved the story for the western imagination. Perhaps that's why the queue for *Peter Pan's Flight* in Disneyland—where John got his start—extends forever into Fantasyland where people love the old ride as much as they cherish the story, just like in our little corner of rural Massachusetts. The story, however, has some problems and, as a glance through *The New York Times* illustrates, contemporary productions have met fierce resistance that sometimes result in canceled performances. This was not to be a candy-sweet theme-park ride for us at Oakmont.

Unlike Hook and Peter, Kris and I are the best of friends.

Act I, Scene 3: Jeff

I spent far more of my time as a director managing money and fundraising than creating. Fortunately, the residents of Ashburnham and Westminster support diverse extracurricular learning opportunities from the stage and the art studio to the engineering shop and the athletic fields. For the theatre program, taxpayers fund the director's stipend, maintain the auditorium, and cover the costs of the custodial staff, but the production costs—every penny—must be fundraised each year. Generally, about one-third of the revenue comes from ticket sales, another third comes from advertisement sales in the playbill, and the remainder comes from various fundraisers like pancake breakfasts, small arts grants, and t-shirt sales. Long before Maura pulled the hook from the box I had talked with ZFX Effects of Louisville, Kentucky who would handle the stage flying. I needed to know from the start if we could even afford the flying effects with our shoestring budget. Adding the flying expenses as well as a special fourth performance of the show for children increased the budget of *Peter Pan* roughly $10,000 over both *Grease* and *The Sound of Music*. On the one hand, plenty of people who work in the private sector easily make a $10,000 bonus each year. For us, we looked for that $10,000 in meatballs at spaghetti suppers and pancakes generously flipped by members of the town Lions Clubs. The goal felt manageable, although like climbing a small mountain.

Producing an authentic *Peter Pan* necessitated the flying expense, but I elected to take on the fundraising challenge for the complimentary children's show. So why do it? J. M. Barrie's dedication to children has been well documented elsewhere, particularly dramatized in the film and stage productions of *Finding Neverland* when, on opening night—December 27, 1904—he set aside seats for orphan children. Today, Great Ormond Street Hospital for Children in London retains the rights to *Peter Pan* from Barrie's bequest. *Peter Pan* mostly reads like a story for children, but especially a story for children in need, and a fraction of every ticket sold, along with $1 from the sale of each copy of *Flight School*, returns to the hospital. Sure, by producing the musical Oakmont students became a part of that legacy, but by throwing open the doors, for at least one special performance for children, we would truly live the spirit of the show rather than just acknowledge it.

I knew from earlier productions that the Cultural Councils in both Ashburnham and Westminster would likely support such a project for school children, especially if I could share the cost between several funders. The town Lions Clubs have always been generous to Oakmont Theatre, and between them and the Councils, I stitched together the majority of the funding for the children's performance—but not all. To cover the musicians and royalties for that one performance I needed to break $3000, and an additional grand would ease both my budget and my mind. I avoided tapping existing revenue streams like advertisers because I relied on them for other costs. On Wednesday of the week—remember, Kris gave me a week to sort it out—I emailed Chris Wells, an Oakmont alumnus who raised three kids in the schools and works with several local charitable foundations. I told him my idea which neatly divided the cost between six groups at $600 each. His response for the David B. Wells Memorial Fund read: "Fantastic Jeff! I love the plan and your vision. I'm in for the $600 and up to $1,000 if you end up needing it." Assuming the other funders would agree—and they did—we had a children's show completely free to elementary school families for April 26.

Kris teaches in classroom 421 and I taught in 417, just two doors down the hall. Around 7:30 each night, although we worked together all day, we would often text each other, which turned into a couple of laughs. This became one of my favorite virtual conversations that spring:

A twelve-piece professional orchestra with harp, plus a pianist, for four shows and two rehearsals, bears a significant price and I knew I had to raise serious money for this production. By chance, in the corridor after the curtain fell on *Grease*, I met a student's dad who eagerly reached for my hand.

Phenomenal job, Mr. A. Great stuff.

Thank you. The kids are amazing. Are you here for a student?

I'm Max's dad. Leon, please, he said handing me his card. *I'd love to help with refreshments.*

That would be great, I said, seeing his card as a sales representative for a food distributor.

I don't know what you think, but we could do lots with food.

I thought similarly, but could not have imagined the fundraising, or my friendship, that developed with Leon Charbonneau.

For me, the school year never winds down. We all race to the finish line, pausing at the Evening With the Arts, the spring concert, myriad Commencement celebrations, and then come to a jolting halt. After my trip to California, my attention turned to end-of-year tasks and final exams. The perusal score and script for *Peter Pan* arrived and I brought them home for summer vacation which, along with my old copy of *Peter and Wendy,* started my summer reading. I prepared my teaching materials for fall, including articles and maps that I use to discuss Native American history. I knew from my early thinking that a significant problem of racial stereotyping existed in the 1904 story; thankfully, I had the summer to sort it out. Kris often remarks, and I agree, that we need to imagine every show in our own way, for our community. Understanding the stereotyping problem in *Peter Pan* became part of my imagination that summer.

As the finale faculty lunch ended, and teachers said their goodbyes like teens, Kris gave me a farewell hug, although I'm sure we texted within the hour.

Enjoy your cruise, I said.

Did I tell you what's playing on-board?

Nope. Anything Goes? South Pacific?

CATS.

It's a sign, Kris.

I'll quit if you ever ask me to conduct CATS, he reminded me.

I grinned like Rum Tum Tugger before saying: *Make sure you find a harpist before you leave.*

Top priority. I even bet there's one on the ship.

We hugged and smiled as we walked toward the sunlight and feeling the freedom of summer as if we had never grown up.

I cracked open the cover of *Peter Pan* that afternoon. The story of the boy Peter—on stage, on screen, and in the adapted novel *Peter and Wendy*—begins as many remember in the sanctuary of the Darling nursery, where many of us, if not all, want to belong. Yet, danger violates the security of the home even before the story begins, for the title of the first chapter, "Peter Breaks Through," hints of a Neverland beyond filled with pirates, crocodiles, and people called Indians. In *Peter Pan*, we encounter something other than a lullaby.

The introduction to Barrie's Indians, however, startles the reader: "On the trail of the pirates, stealing noiselessly down the war-path, which is not visible to inexperienced eyes, come the redskins, every one of them with his eyes peeled. They carry tomahawks and knives, and their naked bodies gleam with paint and oil," Barrie wrote. "Strung around them are scalps, of boys as well as of pirates, for these are the Piccaninny tribe, and not to be confused with the softer-hearted Delawares or the Hurons." Tiger Lily emerges from among them as the most memorable of the braves. Barrie described her as "proudly erect, a princess in her own right. She is the most beautiful of dusky Dianas and the belle of the Piccaninnies, coquettish, cold and amorous by turns; there is not a brave who would not have the wayward thing to wife, but she staves off the altar with a hatchet" (67). I already knew Barrie's 1904 description of indigenous Americans did not align with the contemporary values of our community, and re-reading that passage again in 2017 confirmed my belief.

The Edwardian world of J. M. Barrie existed just forty years after the Massacre at Sand Creek in Colorado Territory, where the militia killed 200 Cheyenne and Arapaho, most of whom were women and children. At the Battle of Wounded Knee in South Dakota, the U.S. Army slew 300 Lakotas just fourteen years before *Peter Pan* first flew onto the London stage—a boy in the audience might have been born that same year. George, the oldest of the Llewelyn Davies boys whose story has been dramatized in *Finding Neverland*, was three at the time of the battle—such contemporary slaughters served as the tragic backdrop against which Barrie set the Indians of *Peter Pan*. Not only were U.S.-Indian relations tragic at the turn of the century, so were the caricatures of native life like those written by Barrie. Still, I struggled to believe the historical circumstances of 1904 that influenced Barrie's writing condemned the entire work, especially with its universal values of bravery, adventure, innocence, and friendship. So began my 2017 summer reading.

These ideas were not new to me. My graduate research in history examined the ways and ends to which early modern Euro-Americans described the indigenous peoples of the Western Hemisphere, found in sources ranging from Las Casas's *Destruction of the Indies* to the hysteria of Mary Rowlandson's captivity narrative—a story local to central Massachusetts—to the more analytic *Relations* of the French Jesuits or Rousseau's *Discourse on Inequality.* Reading Barrie's fiction brought me back to the essential questions of my graduate work: in what ways did Barrie describe "Indians?" To what end did he use those descriptions in the children's story? For this project, did the genre of storybook differ from the intent of a colonial pamphlet? I reread my thesis alongside *Peter and Wendy*, and I opened Edward Said's *Orientalism* to rethink the problem of "the other." While I knew *Peter Pan* to be timeless and loved, I also believed theatre, especially high school theatre, becomes a safe harbor for ideas. As I reread Barrie's description of his "Indians," I became more concerned. I text Kris in times of crisis, like this.

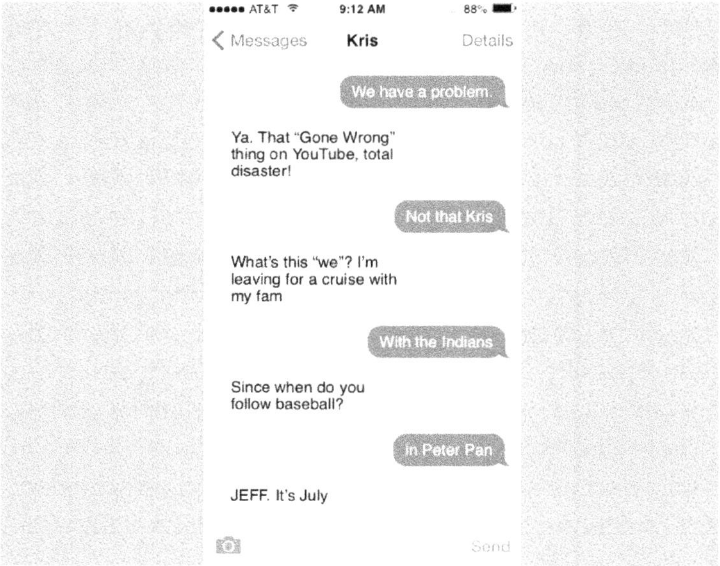

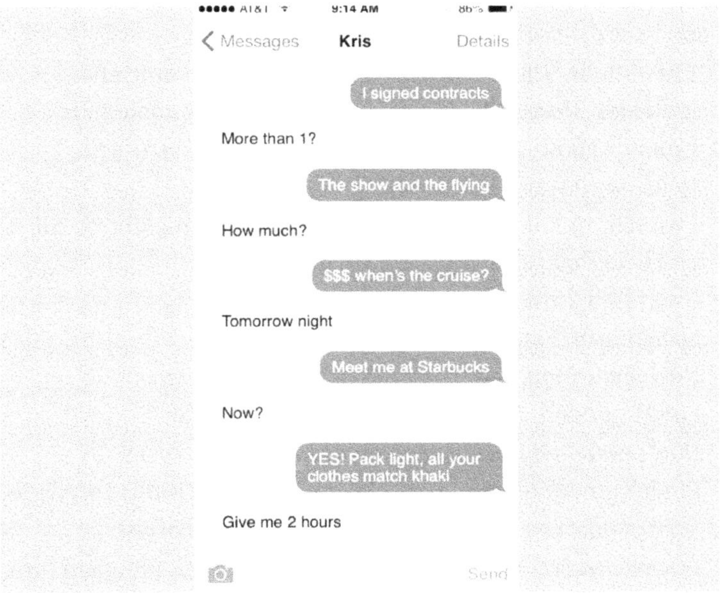

When Kris arrived, he had replaced his school necktie with cargo shorts and red sox jersey, presenting him as "Vacation Kris." His venti cold brew with vanilla sweet cream waited for him on the table.

What's the problem? he started, *Don't say Peter Pan is a girl.*

Look, I handed him my phone with a *New York Times* headline on the screen: "A School Cancels 'Peter Pan,' Calling it Offensive to Indians." *I'll send you the link.*

Yeah, do, he said, handing it back. *Will you pull the plug?*

There's got to be a way to do this. There are more than 150 productions scheduled in the United States this year. It's not like we're the only ones. Leominster is staging it in December, I said, referring to the neighboring city. *It's also playing at North Shore Music Theatre, and they're professionals.*

Maybe they'll ask us how we did it, he said, making me laugh.

I don't see the problem.

The Indians. They're written like comic book characters.

It's a kids' story, Jeff. Kids also don't fly—think about that.

I know, I know. I just don't want controversy, I stressed.

How are you going to avoid it?

I wanted to talk it through with you, first. I'm going to call a friend who's a history professor for her ideas.

Great idea; I'll focus on the music.

Speaking of, I started.

I'm on vacation, this better not be a harp question.

Fair. I nodded. *Did you get good seats for CATS?*

Don't ever, and I mean ever, ask me to conduct CATS.

But it's got everything, Kris.... he stood up and interrupted me.

Sorry, I gotta go. I'm interviewing a potential harpist.

Have a good cruise with your parents, my friend. I hugged him. *It'll be good to be with them.*

Inclusion, family, and friendship are all at the heart of the Neverland story, like when the Lost Boys (and Girls) playfully build a house—and an adoptive family—for Wendy. When Nibs asked Wendy if she was pleased, she called the work a "Lovely, darling house." The orphaned children longed for family, as Barrie wrote: '"And we are your children,' cried the twins. Then all went on their knees, and holding out their arms cried, 'O Wendy lady, be our mother"' (89). In the Neverland story, the children played at being a family; and, just as the donors envisioned a special, inclusive children's performance at Oakmont, I also wanted to ensure that everyone, like the Lost Boys (and Girls), could feel a part of the story—whether on stage or not. A recent Oakmont graduate handed me the ideal opportunity to foster greater inclusion that summer.

I taught Mimi in history class, and it surprised me after several weeks of classes to learn that she preferred Mimi to her birth name of Emma. *There were three Emmas in my kindergarten class, I needed to be different*, she told me. I was equally surprised when she auditioned for *Grease*.

Have you ever been on stage before? I asked.

Just little kid dance. But the school cut cheering this winter because of the budget and I have nothing to do, can I join?

Of course, I said.

While Kris and I hold auditions, it's only to cast and not to cut. Kris and I find room on the Oakmont stage for anyone who commits to a show. Not only Mimi joined the cast for *Grease*, but so too did her best friend Clarisse whom I cast as a Pink Lady. Mimi brought both dance and attitude with her, and she made a very convincing Cha-Cha, who was known as "the best dancer at Saint Bernadette's." Apparently, both girls loved the experience and, after the show, I asked Mimi to write about her experience as a senior. She wrote, "While I can't say my singing or acting has improved a whole lot (it might be a hopeless cause), the musical has bolstered my confidence and happiness in a totally new way. I feel confident that I am able to go onto a stage full of my friends and perform my heart out, a feat I imagined would be more difficult upon first signing-up." She also spoke to her inclusion as a cast member: "The spring musical is a beautifully inclusive place; I truly feel every individual would be able to find a belonging place there. The musical provides a place for everyone to be accepted for who they are. This activity fosters love, enthusiasm, and acceptance and I am lucky to have experienced it." After Oakmont, Mimi worked as an *au pair* in Paris before entering the Global Scholars program at American University. We met at Starbucks just before she left for Paris and we talked about *Peter Pan.*

I wish the HOPE House kids could see that, she said.

What's HOPE House?

I volunteered there. It's for city kids who need, well, hope.

You volunteered there all year and I never knew? I asked.

Well yeah, why brag? She smiled while I thought.

Where is it?

Not far, in Gardner.

I'll get them there, Mimi.

Really? Omygosh.

Let me work on it. Go be great in Paris. Bon voyage.

I asked around about HOPE House and I found they were a great organization with which to partner. The House of Peace and Education in Gardner dates to the late 1960s as a mission of the Sisters of Saint Joseph. As a nonprofit organization "with an interfaith spirit," they enjoy "the financial and moral support of virtually every faith community in Gardner" and beyond. Today they provide youth and teens after school programming as well as job readiness and training—a truly inspirational group that does much good in the recovering industrial city (read more at hopegardner.org). I learned several Oakmont groups, including Students Against Destructive Decisions and the Student Council, worked regularly with HOPE House. Inviting sixty or so members of HOPE House to the matinee posed few problems beyond finding tickets for them, but I perceived obstacles beyond ticket prices. Although Gardner borders Ashburnham, we needed to provide transportation to the group if we offered tickets. I also suspected that some, if not all, of the HOPE guests would appreciate lunch before the show. My mind continued to turn as the clock of summer vacation quickly wound down.

I had included a similar group of Oakmont students at the 2017 production of *Grease*. For several years, a private donor gave money to help the program in any way possible, and I used the funds to purchase tickets for members of the Oakmont Friends Club to enjoy the show. Friends Club fosters inclusion and inspiration at Oakmont as the group's advisors—Mrs. Brittany Smeltekop and her colleagues in the Special Education department—plan outings that pair students of diverse ability and reinforce the bonds of friendship. Using these donated funds for the Friends Club both supported the actors on stage and the kids of the Friends Club to appreciate each other in the murkiness of adolescence. I've learned much about the work and mission of the Friends Club as more of its members become active on stage. They're not unlike Barrie's Lost Boys (and Girls) as they band themselves together for support. Some of the members—just like the Lost Boys (and Girls)—are quite vulnerable, and thankfully there's a Peter or a Wendy (like Brittany) to guide them.

At the end of *Peter Pan*, Mr. and Mrs. Darling not only joyfully welcome their three children home, but despite their thin wallet, they make room for the Lost Boys (and Girls), too. We tried, like the Darlings, to include everyone on our journey. In reaching out to the elementary school students, the Native American community, the friends at HOPE House, and the Friends Club, I wanted to invite everyone to Neverland.

For as long as I could remember, my family has been associated with a local group called the Beacon of Hope; it's a respite program for adults with intellectual disabilities. My great aunt, Iris, enjoyed the programs at the Beacon for many years and I, along with my family, often participated in their annual walk-a-thon. I emailed the Executive Director Vicki Briggs asking if families at the Beacon could use thirty tickets or so, if they provided their own transportation. She jumped at the offer, requiring me to set aside another thirty seats the Saturday matinee. Kris had rightly asked who would pay for HOPE House and I hadn't figured that out yet, nor did I have an exact plan for the guests from the Beacon. The terms of the licensing agreement coupled with the cost of the orchestra made it clear I couldn't give the seats away for free. I seemed to be making—rather than solving—problems for myself. Walking in the New England woods that summer, I tried not to worry about money like Mr. Darling; instead, I sought to restore my energy before the new academic year began. *Mimi*, I thought. *This all started with her. I'll need her help to pull this off, even from Paris.* I knew I had only six months, maybe even seven, to work out the details.

I also thought more about branding as fall arrived. We needed a unique logo for the production, something to capture the spirit of not only the show but also the spirit of the journey. With a nudge from Larry Szalay, the graphic arts teacher, I reached out to Steph, whom I knew from class and who had just begun—as an upperclassman—to become involved in theatre. I explained to her that I needed a simple image, maybe with the phrase "never grow up." Most importantly, I didn't want Peter as the elvish figure of Disney or even Mary Martin. Our Peter looked like a frustrated teenager who didn't fit into the world. "With messy hair," I told her. In short order, Steph sent me some great sketches. One, in particular, had a teenage Peter with messy hair sitting in a circle, as if he sat on the edge of the moon. She captured him perfectly and we put him on everything: pens, notebooks, t-shirts, posters, the playbill, and even sunglasses—as a teenager, our Peter didn't want to grow up and the world of adults left him frustrated. Our Peter searched for his place—whether in Neverland, or the Darlings' nursery, or even Oakmont, and Steph captured that search and apprehension in her logo. Even today, it reminds me that we saw Neverland differently at Oakmont than other schools had. More importantly, by reaching out to Steph, I included another student who might not otherwise participate in the musical program—reinforcing not only my talk of inclusion but also the practice Kris and I emphasized. I knew, however, despite all my positive and inclusive rhetoric, I needed much more than pixie dust and lovely thoughts to lift this increasingly-complex production off the auditorium stage.

Original "never grow up" logo designed by Steph S.

Act I, Scene 4: Dave

Since sitting in Mrs. Phyllis Price's 1985 Kindergarten class at the now-demolished Ashburnham Veterans Memorial School, I went back to school—in one way or another—in every September for thirty-four years. I don't remember dreading the return either as a student or a teacher, and I was often quite excited to go, but in September of 2017, preparing for Peter Pan's arrival at Oakmont challenged me greatly. Barrie wrote that the Lost Boys (and Girls) all went to school after their adoption but, "Before they had attended school a week they saw what goats they had been not to remain on the island; but it was too late now, and soon they settled down to being as ordinary as you or me..." (210). School made the children normal, almost like cogs in the wheel of Mr. Darling's industrial world. As a teacher and as a theatre director, I tried to share my back-to-school enthusiasm with the kids, enliven my classroom and the stage, and get to the real, creative work of reading, writing, and imagining. Just like for the Lost Boys (and Girls) however, boring chores often got in the way of creative growth.

Dave Lantry, Oakmont engineering teacher, similarly returned to school each September for most of his adult life between 1980 and 2018. On the one hand, Dave is something of a mad scientist—loved by students across the school for his energy and ability to make things (safely) explode. He looks just like Doc Brown from *Back to the Future*: tall, thin, and with a shock of white hair, undoubtedly colored by the many crazy things he's done. On the other hand, Dave is also the model dad of three daughters and an enthusiastic grandfather. Domesticity balances his 'madness,' a domestic life that mirrors Mr. Darling. Barrie introduces Mr. Darling to us calculating expenses as a clerk and trying to make ends meet: "I have one pound seventeen here, and two and six at the office; I can cut off my coffee at the office, say ten shillings, making two nine and six..." (3). The industrial revolution that ushered Mr. Darling into clerical office work and middle-class living had, as Barrie pointed out, deprived him and so many others of the innocence of childhood; and, while Dave is the consummate child-at-heart his life was also altered by industrial technology. Dave remains a nurturing dad not only to his family but to all of Oakmont, along with his wife, June, who headed the Oakmont Special Education department. So many students and teachers looked to them both as parents.

I, too, felt the financial burden of Mr. Darling sitting with his ledger; indeed, rising money for a high school musical felt just as overwhelming. The price tag for the two previous shows—*The Sound of Music* and *Grease*—hovered around $20,000 for the weekend, but calculating additional costs for *Peter Pan* with a larger orchestra, more costumes, and flying, bloated the budget to $30,000 or so. I often sat like Mr. Darling, but at Starbucks, scanning my spreadsheets to find money I could borrow to lift the project off the ground, or more accurately, keep it airborne.

On the Monday after *Grease* closed, Dave pulled me aside

in the teacher's room and, with his typical enthusiasm, said: *making kids fly to Neverland is going to cost a pretty penny. I have an idea.* Dave proceeded to explain how Oakmont hosted the annual VEX robotics competition every May, attracting student teams from across New England. Traditionally, one of the other engineering teachers—John DeCicco, also a longtime Oakmont Theatre supporter—grilled hamburgers and hotdogs for the 150 competitors at cost, but John retired in 2015 and they needed a cook. *Make it a fundraiser*, Dave said. *Figure your costs and set a fair price—it's a win-win.*

Kris will tell you I can't even feed myself; I was always the most regular customer in the school cafeteria. I can't make lunch for two never mind two hundred, but I had just made the acquaintance of Leon Charbonneau and since he had mentioned food sales in our hallway conversation, I thought he could help me help the robotics students. I texted him:

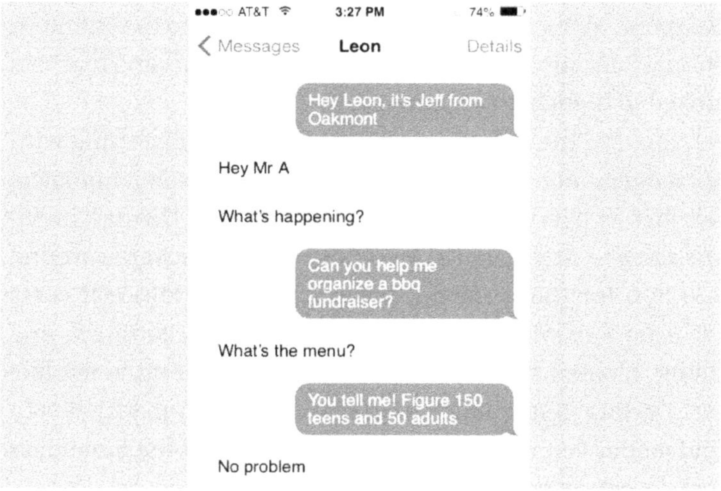

Leon organized hamburgers, veggie burgers, and hotdogs with

chips, water, and fresh-baked cookie. We learned lots from that first meal—enough to fill a textbook. In the following two years, Leon staged almost a dozen of these lunches, mostly for teachers on early-release days but also annually for the VEX competition. We only served hamburgers and hotdogs the one time; in 2018 we served pulled barbecued chicken sandwiches with cheddar cheese, chips, coleslaw, ice cream sandwich, and water for $7 and in 2019 we offered a hot meatball sub with mozzarella, pasta salad, chips, water, and fresh-baked cookie for the same price. The VEX lunch in May achieved two goals: first, it represented modest fundraising that helped us jump-start the next show; and second, the lunch allowed drama students to assist another group in the school like the robotics students. Oakmont has many active service organizations: the Student Council, National Honor Society, Students Against Destructive Decisions, and Peer Leaders, but for all the fundraising of the Drama Club, theatre students also needed to give back to their peers beyond what they give on stage. Providing the VEX lunch represented a small way to foster this service. The projects would have been impossible without Leon's expertise and the dedication of parents like Diane Leger and Laurie Ellsworth as well as Keith and Lisa Aubin.[6] I have joked that we stage theatre one meatball and one pancake at a time and it's rooted in fact. Little did I envision the gratitude I would have for Leon, these parents, and especially Dave and his students, as we prepared *Peter Pan*.

Leon proved instrumental in fundraising with his gourmet lunches throughout the 2017-2018 season. While students loved the VEX lunch, I knew the faculty would be a harder sell. I aimed for a fantastic start to the new school year and planned to feed the teachers on the first day before the students arrived. No matter what I asked of Leon, his response is always "no problem." That August we served up a lunch of freshly-grilled chicken Caprese sandwiches with a sweet strawberry shortcake ending. In September, at a professional day lunch for just teachers, Leon laid on a hearty spaghetti lunch with meatballs, good enough to make your grandmother ask for the recipe. The teachers raved at the freshness and quality, and at only $8, they loved the value. I didn't want to gouge anyone on lunch and, more often than not, the teachers left a Hamilton. Members of the cast and some parents always helped serve and clean. Over the course of the year, we raised $2,000 from these combined lunches, and I eventually found a special project for that lunch money.

Schools in Massachusetts are usually closed to students on Election Day in November as many operate as polling stations, but remain open to teachers for a workday. Dave and June anticipated their retirement that year and came to me with a proposal for the November lunch: the drama club would run the lunch as a fundraiser, but Dave and June would fry up their world-famous fish, with the profits going to *Peter Pan.*

I love it, I said to Dave, *I'll arrange everything. You get the fish.*

You bet. I'll get an assload of fish, Dave replied grinning.

On that crisp first Tuesday of November, Dave and I arrived at school early and erected garden tents outside so that all the frying could be done *al fresco*. The fish luncheon worked perfectly as Dave preferred to fry fish rather than sit in collegial workshops and it also relieved Leon and the small, but dedicated, group of parent volunteers of a day of meal preparations. Dave brought three propane-fueled plumbers furnaces, ten gallons of oil, and, you guessed it, an assload of fish. Folding work tables became laden with eggs, batter, and fish—this was no amateur production—and by lunchtime, he served an impressive catch with help from his colleagues in the Engineering department. After everyone had their fill, two giant pans of fried fish remained with a mountain of coleslaw.

I hate the waste, Dave said, *but you can't run out—even if it means a smaller profit. The fishes and loaves story was in the Bible because of the leftovers, not a shortage, just like the wine. Jesus always made extra.*

Don't worry about that, I have a plan. I called Our Father's House, a local shelter for homeless men, and explained what we had. The manager said the guys would feast on fish that night. I felt good about this; while much of my fundraising demanded that I ask people to give the production money, it was important for me, the kids, and the program as a whole, to share what we could. If making a smaller profit from the fish lunch meant sharing our abundance with those who had less, well, that's the sort of work Oakmont Theatre—and Dave and June Lantry—are all about.

On Wednesday I walked to the engineering shops searching for Dave. I write "shops" because the twenty-first century shops include two computer labs (including one for video game design), a robotics lab, as well as space for woodworking, metalworking, and a studio for two 3-D printers. This isn't the mid-century Industrial Arts department of *Grease*; no, in the shop mature girls and boys—not adults—engineer real solutions to contemporary problems.

Captain Dave, I said, extending my hand to shake his.

Did Peter Pan make any money yesterday?

I'm not sure yet, I need the receipt for the fish so I can repay you.

June has it, of course. Ask her.

Thank you, Dave. For everything you always do around here, no matter what program.

We're family, it's what we do, he grinned.

Dave and June have hosted many of these fish fries before, both at school and at their home. Now that they have both retired, they are sorely missed at school although they do make frequent appearances at school events like the VEX competition and the musical.

Let us know how else we can help with the show, Dave added.

I need a ship, Dave. A swashbuckling ship for Captain Hook. The Jolly Roger of all Jolly Rogers, I said.

Yo ho. Methinks you do need a ship, he said with wide eyes.

Dave Lantry, hosting his famous backyard fish fry.

I did not know Dave well when I returned to teach at Oakmont in 2011. Although he had taught there since the early 1980s, he took a ten-year contracting hiatus when I studied at Oakmont. I knew of him, but it wasn't until my second year that we became good friends. While I never envisioned returning to Oakmont, I didn't hesitate when Mr. Uminski asked me to fill the librarian position held by the ailing Mr. Tom Anderson. One of my first assignments came when Mr. U. asked me, along with Diane Erickson, the head of the English department and my Advanced Placement (A.P.) Literature teacher, to coordinate a school-wide summer reading program in 2012. *Something to bring the whole school together around a book*, Mr. Uminski had said. Diane had spearheaded similar summer reading initiatives in the past, but the "one school, one book" nature of this idea set it apart from the previous models. We reviewed book lists and solicited ideas from the faculty, and finally chose *I Am the Cheese*, by local author Robert Cormier for the 2012 read. We left it to each homeroom teacher to plan class-specific activities. The culminating activity day in September worked fairly well but wasn't a blockbuster—until Dave and his students rode their bicycles through the corridors reenacting the hero's bike ride through Massachusetts, raising the stakes for more awe-inspiriting activities the next year.

In 2013, we put some titles to the students who picked *Treasure Island*, probably because almost everyone likes a pirate story. We all departed school that June ready to read Robert Louis Stevenson but without much of an end-goal in mind. Diane and I only had a vague idea about what sorts of activity, if any, to do in September to unify the school. Faculty feedback clearly pointed to a desire to energize the school with some really dynamic activities—something along the lines of Dave's bike ride.

Early that September, Dave walked into the library.

Good summer, Jeff?

Yes, how was Vermont, Dave?

Boring.

I found this hard to believe; Dave clearly kept himself active.

I hurt myself water skiing, I was on the couch all summer.

That sucks, Dave.

Ya, it did. But it gave me time to read Treasure Island. It's an adventure, you know.

From there began a discussion of how to turn Oakmont Regional High School into an adventure theme park to celebrate summer reading, complete with maps, treasures, quizzes, puzzles, and costumes. We worked hard to create Summer Reading Day, which consumed a great amount of time and resources, but which we all fondly remember in many different ways. The project became my introduction to working with Dave—learning how best to harness his unending enthusiasm and energy. *Treasure Island* Day (or Pirate Day as we called it) never had a ship, so Dave's offer to dream up a *Jolly Roger* for Captain Hook became a beautiful bookend to our professional friendship. I earmarked the money from the fish fry and the other faculty lunches to build 'Captain Davie's' ship. In time, I dropped the Captain and began calling him Admiral, and I never forgot that the journey of building Captain Hook's *Jolly Roger* started with a fish—or as Dave said, *an assload of fish.*

Also that fall, I met Carrie Tobia at Starbucks. Carrie teaches grade 8 English at Overlook Middle School and I've taught both her sons in A.P. U.S. History; I also consider her a good friend. During the previous summer, she helped me edit another piece of writing and we looked to the new school year as we mused about school life over coffee.

How's your school year? I asked.

Rough start, but they'll adjust. You?

It's all Peter Pan. I changed the alarm on my phone to be a harp. I wake up and think about it.

How's the show going? Carrie asked, always enthusiastic.

I told her about the HOPE House and the Beacon of Hope projects.

That's really great; Geoffrey has to get involved in that, she said, mentioning her older son.

What do you mean?

He and his buddies should help—can they? What do you—what do those kids—need?

I need money for a bus to get the kids from Gardner. Like $200.

That's not a ton of money, she said.

Maybe your boys could raise it, maybe with National Honor Society or something?

Done, she said. *They'll do it*, and she winked.

The opportunity to raise money for a bus presented itself shortly thereafter when I received an email from Mary Waight of Westminster. Mrs. Waight served as a school administrator in a neighboring district and is the wife of our former principal, Bill, as well as the mother of an alumna. Mary also heads the Westminster Cultural Council. Few members of our community are as closely connected to our school as Mary. I also learned from her message that she belonged to a small group at the Westminster Congregational Church known as the Women's Fellowship, who meet monthly to discuss topics of timely interest. She asked if I would facilitate their September 2017 Fellowship discussion on the Constitution. Unfortunately, I was unavailable that night; however, I proposed a student panel that I could coach in advance to facilitate the discussion. I had every confidence that a group of seniors—all of whom had completed my A.P. U.S. History class and many of whom belonged to the National Honor Society—could do the job well. She agreed and I made all the arrangements. The kids saw me in homeroom the morning after their successful presentation. Not only had the evening gone well, they said, but the Fellowship had given them a check for $100. "For the bus," one boy said shyly as he handed me an envelope.

That's half the amount right there, I said. *Thank you.*

We know. Just another hundred to go, said Geoff.

A week before the October Homecoming Pep Rally, this same group of boys appeared in my classroom after school. I enjoyed teaching them in A.P. U.S. History as juniors, and now they were big seniors with golden hearts. They wanted to talk about the bus for the HOPE House kids, with a plan to sell numbered tennis balls for $1 each that students could throw at me on the football field during the pep rally. I'd be dressed as Peter Pan, complete with green tights. The thrower of the closest ball would win a donated gift card from Dunkin' Donuts. The project had easy math: with 100 balls plus the honorarium from the Women's Fellowship they would reach their goal of $200. The kids executed the plan brilliantly: the balls easily sold at lunches and the school saw me in green tights. Kris even had the marching band play Darth Vader's Imperial March as I walked on to the field to make me a target worth hitting and, while I don't remember whose ball came closest, there's a video of the event on jeffreywaubuchon.com.

Municipalities in Massachusetts annually receive money from

the state's Cultural Council to fund local arts programming and Oakmont Theatre—along with numerous other school and local programs—has benefited greatly from generous grants awarded by both the Ashburnham and Westminster councils. Because the grant deadline comes in October, I had to form my vision for the grant application over the summer. *Peter Pan* provided me with a clear idea: I requested $600 from each town towards the children's performance and demonstrated effective cost-sharing with the Lions Clubs and the Wells Foundation. I titled the project "Including Families in Peter Pan," and both towns generously funded the request. I extended the request to the councils of nearby Gardner ($160) and Leominster ($140) to help subsidize the tickets for the HOPE House group and guests from the Beacon of Hope. The councils agreed and supported the project; with their funding, they helped ensure we included our friends from these organizations at the show.

Another local and generous funder, the Ashburnham-Westminster Foundation for Academic Excellence (AWFAE)—a citizen-led non-profit group—raises private funds to support teaching and learning as well as implement innovative ideas that enhance the lives of public-school children in Ashburnham and Westminster. AWFAE funds requests for equipment and technology beyond the scope of the school district's budget, like 3-D printers in the Engineering department, and that "raise the bar" on educational achievement, but does not buy tickets like the cultural councils. I pitched two ideas to the AWFAE board in the hope that they would pick one. I wrote a small grant to purchase the video recording license for *Peter Pan* and to work with the local community access television station, AWCA-TV, as well as the high school TV production club to professionally record and archive the show. AWFAE funded this project with $200. A larger project involved hiring a professional artist to work with the students on set design and construction. The AWFAE board agreed to this as well and supported the project with $800 to help build the Lost Boys' (and Girls') underground house with a local artist, and the parent of a graduate of Oakmont Theatre, Tom Simahk. Students' active learning and growth through the television and set design initiatives drove these projects, which certainly "raised the bar" of the quality and scope of the theatre program. As with the cultural councils, diverse adults stepped forward with serious contributions in support of the project; but the inherent desire to include as many people as possible in the Neverland experience, I think, became the real motivation for the community's support.

Chris Wells quietly helped behind the scenes of *Peter Pan* from its inception; indeed, he had generously helped me find private funding for the children's show. In addition to the many ways Chris leads in the community, he also serves as the President of AWFAE. A year after *Peter Pan* closed, I asked him to share his observations as a donor, community member, alumnus, and the parent of a student not participating in the show. He wrote, "Sitting in the audience watching the show felt, to me, more like the final line of a great book. Everything that happened before is what made it magical. For the better part of a year, I saw students and the community get involved and become a part of the success of something big—even if they weren't on stage that night." I found good company in Chris as I experienced the excitement for this show, but something moved in the air—maybe pixie dust—that I couldn't capture. The excitement increased as the school year unfolded and we grew, and the growing suggests we learned.

Also during that school year, we began to say goodbye to Dave and June as they approached retirement. In 2017, the cast dedicated the Saturday night performance of *Grease* to three retiring teachers. The dedication brought many to the Saturday night show to share the moment with these teachers and their families. Given all that Dave and June had done for the program, and especially the fish and what I imagined would be a dramatic ship, dedicating *Peter Pan* to their honor was obvious, but I still put it to the kids who enthusiastically agreed. Never could I have imagined the overwhelming support for the Saturday night performance when I announced its dedication to our own Mr. and Mrs. Darling. June mothered us when we needed it most and, while Dave likes to play it cool, never had Oakmont a more caring dad than him. Across their careers, Mr. and Mrs. Lantry always believed everyone at Oakmont could soar, and our production of a century-old story—that expressed loyalty, friendship, and inclusion—celebrated their belief. Throughout the year I did look to Dave and June as parents; they fed me when I was hungry, encouraged me when I was frustrated, and the built our set in a way that mirrored their own personalities: able to weather the roughest storm with stability and strength. I needed Dave and June just as much as I needed Kris and John to pull the show together and I remain ever-grateful for their continued friendship today.

Act I, Scene 5: Jeff

"The moment you doubt whether you can fly, you cease for ever to be able to do it," wrote J. M. Barrie in his 1902 story, *The Little White Bird*, which included the first published reference to Peter Pan. I often doubted myself during the fall of 2017 as I applied for a Mass Humanities grant to fund some of the educational learning components of the production. A colleague connected me with Dr. Robert Goodby who teaches anthropology at Franklin Pierce College—just across the New Hampshire border from Oakmont—and has supervised excavations of the surrounding Monadnock region for thirty years. He seemed to be the right scholar for this project. From our first email exchange that summer, Bob Goodby and I read from the same page; we similarly understood the problem of Native American stereotyping and sought a practical, rather than theoretical, solution for our New England community. He agreed that Mass Humanities might fund some of the work and encouraged me to begin writing. I kept him informed as I drafted ideas and, more than anything, he confirmed them rather than steer me in a different direction. He acknowledged from the start that, like so many others, he had no real knowledge of *Peter Pan* or the stage but was eager to be a part of the work. A degree of novelty, I learned, existed in our project.

That summer I also studied with Dr. James Stanley of the Theatre, Music, and Dance department at Harvard in a course entitled, "Realism and the Theatre of the Avant-Garde." Many of the ideas about representation in *Peter Pan* took shape in that class. I waited until after the course ended to invite Dr. Stanley to share in the project work—an invitation he graciously accepted. In late July, I composed a Letter of Intent to Mass Humanities, asking them to fund an educational project for the students that would bring scholars like Dr. Goodby and Dr. Stanley, with members of the Native American community, to help the students and adults of Oakmont understand and address the problem of racial stereotyping in *Peter Pan*. I proposed outreach components for the project as well as work on costumes and a post-matinee community discussion forum. Both Dr. Goodby and Dr. Stanley agreed that the idea had merit and encouraged me to apply for the fall funding cycle. Whereas Bob would advise on the problem of historical accuracy and prejudice, James would help us understand "representation" on stage, that is, how to present an old idea more sensitively to a contemporary audience. The application consumed a great amount of my summer, but I believed—and my colleagues agreed—represented the right course of action, and so I flew towards it like Neverland.

I wanted scholars, members of the Native American community, and residents of Ashburnham and Westminster to help us at Oakmont understand this real problem of racial stereotyping on stage. I believed, then and now, the idea represented sound teaching for my students. Kris DeMoura, Bob Goodby, and James Stanley all agreed, along with my colleague Dana Altobelli who chairs the Social Studies department. The project, wholly separate from my duties of producing a high school musical, challenged me just as much as staging the show.

When resistance to the Humanities project first emerged that fall, I jotted down some ideas for those involved. I sought a common vocabulary about our mission: "We at Oakmont, like other groups, believe there are timeless values in *Peter Pan* that speak to audiences today: the innocence of youth, the triumph of good, and the beauty of imagination," I wrote. "We also recognize—and are addressing—the inappropriate portrayal of Native Americans in the 1904 story that does not align with the values of our community." I struggled to understand how anyone could oppose the work, but some did—and strongly. While I didn't meet Bob Goodby in person until February, our early, active email exchange always reminded me that he shared my vision for this project; and, when challenges to the project arose, Bob always helped me to refocus the vision.

According to their mission statement, "Mass Humanities conducts and supports programs that use history, literature, philosophy, and the other humanities disciplines to enhance and improve civic life in Massachusetts" as the state-based affiliate of the National Endowment for the Humanities [NEH]. Per their guidelines, Mass Humanities only funds educational opportunities for actors, not the productions.[7] A glance at their past recipient list didn't show too many high school winners; instead, the projects included mostly colleges, museums, and community groups. I knew my writing needed to focus on learning and civic engagement. My request of $4,615 from Mass Humanities mostly covered the cost of consultants, teaching tools like the authentic tipi and the re-imagined Indian costumes, as well as advertising the post-matinee discussion forum with scholars, Native Americans, students, and the public. As I wrote in the project description, I rejected staging a spaghetti western in our production and instead sought to celebrate the indigenous heritage essential to our shared national identity. "While some schools avoid *Peter Pan* because of its caricature of Native Americans, this is an opportunity to promote an understanding of indigenous culture in our community," I argued. "By directly engaging with Native American members of our community, and adhering to the NEH Code of Ethics, scholars will teach performers about native culture and facilitate face-to-face dialogue about the obligation we owe First Americans...."

The central purpose of the work emphasized dialogue and understanding over caricature and confusion. In addition to the committee's academic members, Kris and Dana both lived and raised their families in Ashburnham and Westminster, so they also saw the project through the eyes of taxpayer residents, knowing well their neighbors' perceptions of the schools. Karen Brown rounded out the team as both an experienced choreographer and also a town resident with grown children, along with school registrar Cathy Stangroom who happily shared her own indigenous history of the Kanai Sioux (from her mother) and the Taino people of the Caribbean (from her father) with the students as part of this committee.

Reaching out into the community, both Jim Eagle and Tammy Bucchino of Westminster willingly shared their perspectives and Native American heritage with us as well. Jim served as a town library trustee for many years and put three children through Oakmont while Tammy, in addition to being a mother, had also graduated from Oakmont with me in 1998. They both took pride in their ancestry and were willing to share it with Oakmont students and their community. As scholars, Bob and James brought excellent credentials to the application, but they lacked the Native American perspective essential to the listening aspect of the project. I found a list of speakers through the Massachusetts Cultural Council who presented on heritage topics to community groups and reached out to Annawon Weedon. A colleague in the Social Studies department recommended Larry Spotted Crow Mann, an interpreter whom she invited into her classes a few years earlier to talk about Native American spirituality. She spoke highly of him and had successfully secured grant funds for his presentation. In their responses, I found the team members enthusiastic about helping us at Oakmont reconcile Barrie's problem for a contemporary audience.

I asked Bob if he had any other contacts of people who consulted on Native American heritage issues and, through a series of forwarded emails and connections, helped me find Madeline Sayet of Uncasville, Connecticut, an award-winning theatre director. According to her website (madelinesayet.com), Ms. Sayet "uses minimalist magical realism to interrogate questions of gendering, indigenous perspectives, and reimagine classic plays to give voice to those who have been silenced." She sounded like a perfect match for the work I envisioned. Things, however, grew heated from this line of inquiry. I still believe everyone involved had the best intentions of not only their respective groups but also Oakmont students; however, in hindsight, I'm not at all certain I adequately explained myself or the project goals.

Ms. Sayet responded first. While I didn't expect the force of her response, in re-reading it, she did offer a different kind of help: "I have seen effective productions where I don't find Tiger Lily offensive but none of them have made her nation a real one, they instead have more depth of character to that fictional nation's story." She wrote. The subsequent text troubled me the most: "Do you have native students at your school or is your plan still to include some form of red face? In which case again I would suggest considering alternative tribes that could be represented in your story that are not Native American. Short story- no I'm not interested in consulting on any project that employs any form of red face." She concluded by leaving the door somewhat ajar, "If you want to think about re-imagining the classics in other ways I could help."

Her provocative "red face" references greatly upset me. I had no intention of staging "red face;" in fact, her comment represented exactly what I sought to avoid. I emailed Bob, feeling pretty low. "These are hot-button issues," he replied "and some of the responses can be like this." He encouraged me to wait for other responses. "I think the key thing here is the option for Native involvement/input. The *Peter Pan* play is by no means specific to Massachusetts, and the stereotypes they employ are pan-Indian (and equally offensive to all, I would think)." So, I waited.

Another email arrived that afternoon from Cheryll Toney Holley, Sonksq (Chief) of the Nipmuc Nation—a state-recognized tribe living in central Massachusetts with a reservation in what is now Grafton, Massachusetts. Her words, like those of Madeline Sayet, aimed to be both instructive and sincere, but as Chief Holley suggested in her last paragraph, "this email is harsh." I quoted the relevant portions for brevity.

> Dear Mr. Aubuchon,
>
> ...Your hope to re-imagine our music, dance, and costumes caused much concern. Our on-going traditional, including drumming and dancing, have

> meaning and purpose, they are not for entertainment, they are not for others to use. We do not wear costumes, we don regalia for ceremony. Please do not re-imagine our lives, past or present....
>
> As the leader of the Nipmuc tribe, I urge you to not carry out your plans to produce the Peter Pan play. We most certainly do not wish that play to be used to 'promote Native American heritage in our central Massachusetts community.' That's not your place, you did not ask us if we wanted you to promote our culture, and it's doubtful that your proposal will do anything other than reinforce the negative perceptions surrounding my people.... I want you to understand that Nipmuc will not support this effort in any way. If you and your school wish to truly learn about my people, then our door is open to you. But not like this.
>
> Aquene,
> Cheryll Toney Holley
> Sonksq (Chief), Nipmuc Nation

I struggled to understand both her objection and Ms. Sayet's. My intention came from a deep desire to do good, not bad. I understood Chief Holley's explanation of the sacredness of drums and regalia, and in no way did I seek to mock that. I searched for a middle ground between a clearly inappropriate motif from 1904 and the reality of indigenous life in central Massachusetts in 2018. I needed a common language, perhaps from a communication coach. In my frustration, Bob suggested I reach out to Dr. Lisa Brooks at Amherst College to try to find a shared vocabulary. I sought dialogue—and others like

Bob, James, and Kris as well as locals like Jim and Tammy saw that—but I couldn't effectively communicate the ideas with these thinkers. Dr. Brooks responded the next day. "Thank you for reaching out with this question. I know Chief Holly well. In addition to being a highly respected leader of an indigenous sovereign nation, she is also well recognized as a deeply knowledgeable tribal historian," Dr. Brooks explained. "She was one of a handful of scholars whom I asked to read and review my forthcoming book in manuscript, because of the depth of her knowledge and her insights on the history and continuance of Native New England. Any advice she gives, I would heed. I see that there is an invitation remaining with her email, so perhaps that is worth considering."

Dr. Brooks's email came as a third strike. Neither she, nor Ms. Sayet, nor Chief Holley knew me. They didn't know how Kris and I sought to build community through theatre at Oakmont. They also didn't know about my graduate work in the field and my sensitivity to the problems of assimilation and acculturation which came not only from books but experienced first-hand as a Peace Corps volunteer in North Africa. Conversely, I didn't know them either and, while I felt mischaracterized, I saw that my suggestion frustrated, if not angered, them. I simply wanted to walk the right path with my students. On the one hand, people in my community whom I respect also recognized this as a road worth walking. Yet, the responses from Ms. Sayet, Chief Holley, and Dr. Brooks suggested I ought not to undertake the journey at all. I turned their words over and over again in my mind. Ms. Sayet accused me of putting "red face" on the high school stage. "As the leader of the Nipmuc tribe," Chief Holley had written, "I urge you to not carry out your plans to produce the Peter Pan play." I appreciated that this leader politely asked me to stop the work; however, everything I had read, studied, and pondered since July told me that this could—and should—be done. Doubt entered my mind in a mammoth way, not just about the grant, but had I lost sight of the ethics of the work?

Take a seat, my friend, Kris said as I walked into his office. I usually sent him copies of emails I wanted to discuss later, and his inbox fills just as full as mine during the marching band season. I had forwarded Dr. Brooks' email as soon as it arrived.

Did I get this wrong?

I don't think so.

How could I be so wrong about this?

I just said I don't think you are.

The emails.

Goodby and Stanley support you. Most importantly, Jim and Tammy support you. Don't the other consultants—Annawon and Larry—support you? The principal and I support you, Jeff.

You're not Chief of the Nipmuc Nation. What if they protest?

I know you're afraid of that, but the people of this community would protect our kids.

True.

Has anyone from town given you pushback against this?

No.

Uminski supports you. The town often supports Mr. Uminski on things like this.

It could get ugly.

What's the worst that could happen?

Picketers.

Besides that.

We don't get the grant.

The money isn't even going to the production, it's just funding all these extra pieces of work and all your extra headaches.

People could still protest. It's happened before.

Enough drama, Jeff—what's the goal? To give the best education to our students, right?

Yes.

So, do you believe that Peter Pan gives our students the best education on stage—yes or no?

Yes. I do. Completely.

Then keep working on it and get out of my office, I have to conduct the concert band.

Contrary to Barrie's admonition to never doubt, I kept doubting myself. Kris, just like Bob Goodby, articulated the right message. I needed more reassurance, however, so I texted John as I walked back down the hall.

At home that night, I reviewed the half-completed grant application. I still needed to define the team of consultants—I surely knew who was a "no"—and demonstrate community support for the project. Over the course of a few weeks, I repeatedly re-examined the problem, even discussing it with my A.P. students. Finally, on October 3, I sent an email to the core group—the people who had been supportive and driving the work since summer. "Despite a rough couple of weeks, and with much input and support from all of you, I'm convinced this project is in the best educational interests of our students and community," I wrote. "I've received just as much support for this work as push-back; but more importantly, the words of support are coming from *within* our community—teachers and parents who have a vested interest in this program. So we're moving forward, hopefully with Mass Humanities funds." The application only needed the community testimonials in addition to the statements of Goodby and Stanley.

I reached out to Bonnie Baer-Simahk. Bonnie had not only graduated from Oakmont and still resided in Ashburnham, but she had also put her two sons through the Oakmont Theatre program—one of which has achieved professional success on Broadway. Although I only made her acquaintance through Kris, I asked her to write a letter of support. "I am aware of Oakmont's longstanding commitment to a strong theatre program, and find the vision for this project particularly compelling," she began. "The audience, and more import, Oakmont students, will be invited to interrogate the derogatory portrayal of Native Americans as this production is traditionally staged, through exploring issues of cultural diversity, ethnic stereotyping, racism and the struggle over historical identity. This promises to be a lively conversation in our small rural town." Megan and Chuck Reitz—Mimi's parents—also supported the project. "We have witnessed firsthand the unique atmosphere of theatre productions at Oakmont, both behind the scenes and on stage," they said. "It gave our children the confidence to take on a role they would not normally have tried and we watched as they quickly turned into 'theatre kids.' To bear witness to the transforming nature of a theatre production is incredible.... All are truly welcome in the Oakmont Theatre department." These testimonials reinvigorated my confidence in both the Humanities project as well as the production. As town residents, the words of Mr. and Mrs. Reitz as well as Ms. Baer-Simahk bolstered the application. On October 18, I clicked "submit." Then, I waited again.

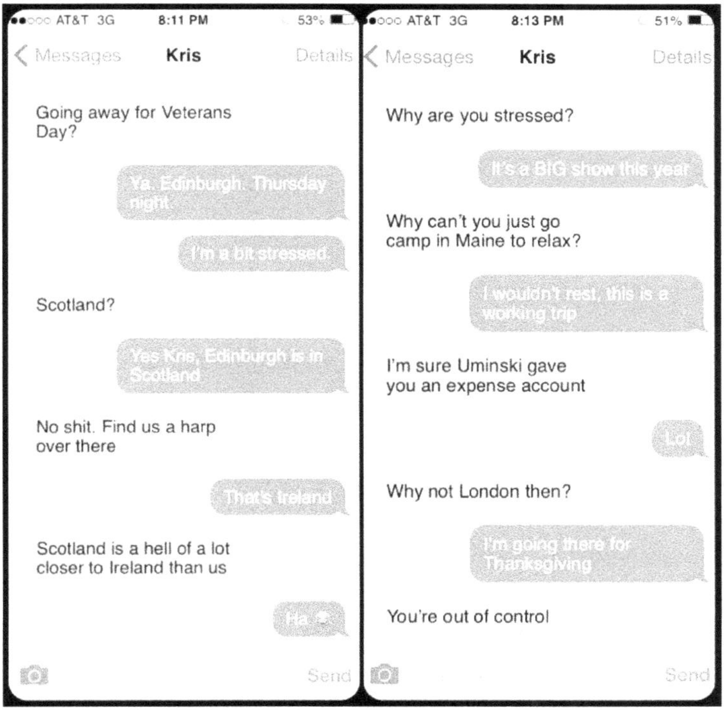

With Veteran's Day 2017 observed on Friday, November 10, we enjoyed a three-day weekend during which I escaped. Edinburgh, however, was neither a random nor a new destination for me as I had enjoyed Thanksgiving there a few years earlier; I liked the city in some ways even more than London. On my previous trip, I headed north by train to Fort William and onto Mallaig via the Glenfinnan Viaduct, which I first saw like so many Americans in *Harry Potter and the Chamber of Secrets.* I didn't have time to explore the Highlands in 2017, but writing and a bit of magic stayed on my mind as I thought about *Peter Pan.* When the curtain fell on the Interclass plays the following weekend, I would live my life in Neverland.

If you positioned Harry Potter fans on a scale of zero to five, with zero indicating no interest in the story and five being the sort of person who keeps a wand on their nightstand in case of Dementors, I'm between a three and a four. I like the stories and the movies—and maybe they spark a little creativity in me—but that's about all. Sure, a strong connection links J. K. Rowling's literary hometown of Edinburgh and her stories, but I just wanted to breathe the Scottish air that J. M. Barrie had in his young adulthood; indeed, Barrie was born and buried in Kirriemur, north of Edinburgh. I didn't visit the grave or the Peter Pan statue in the Angus town center, but someday I will. After studying in Glasgow and Dumfries, Barrie attended the University of Edinburgh where he read literature and wrote drama reviews for the *Edinburgh Evening Courant.* That weekend, I briefly stepped into the collegiate footsteps of Barrie—tiny from what I gather, he measured only 5' 3 ½" tall according to his 1934 passport—before he moved to London and became the playwright who imagined *Peter Pan.*[8]

My red-eye transatlantic flight put me in Edinburgh early Friday morning. With a cloudless blue sky and plenty of fresh air, I walked among the leafless trees in the city with my leather knapsack. My stomach reminded me of a hungry crocodile and, although I knew it's a hotspot for writer-tourists, I've enjoyed eating at The Elephant House, which bears the subtitle "the birthplace of Harry Potter." Rowling created her world in the café where the rear windows overlook Edinburgh Castle, rising like Hogwarts above the city on a giant rock. I sipped a cappuccino and ate a hot breakfast, without the blood pudding. From my pack, I retrieved a little green notebook with Peter Pan on the cover, it's a children's thing really but perfect for keeping my ideas. Eighteen months later, I'm staring at it and its lists of ideas and scratchings inside; most of which came to life. At the bottom of my to-do list, dated 11/10/17, I wrote and underlined *orphan*—it struck me there that both Harry Potter and Peter Pan were orphans, just like Dorothy Gale of Kansas, and they all sought belonging among new friends.

I continued my morning walk from The Elephant House into Greyfriars Kirkyard, embracing the city like Jean Brodie in her prime. I like cemeteries and I find them good for thinking. I found a gravestone mounted to a brick wall and ran my fingers over the scripted words: *"Sacred to the Memory of Thomas Riddell, Esq."* Tom Riddle, who in the story became Harry Potter's nemesis, also grew up as an orphan.

I walked on, enjoying the coolness of November on my face and I headed towards the crowds of the Royal Mile, the road that connects Edinburgh Castle perched high above the city to the Palace of Holyroodhouse, the monarch's official residence in Scotland. The way is dotted with pubs and shops, St. Giles' Cathedral, and a serious statue of Adam Smith (who's buried farther down the Royal Mile in Canongate Kirkyard). Jetlag slowed me and I didn't fancy anything serious as I enjoyed my midday walk. I said a prayer and lit a candle in St. Giles'.

When I emerged into the daylight, I heard a bagpiper playing just down the hill. Stepping into a side street, I entered a sleek shop and bought a hipster pink wool sweater. While I didn't own much pink, I convinced myself I liked the color. When I returned to the street, the piper played louder and a crowd of tourists had gathered to listen. *Tourists*, I thought and walked on.

I returned to a cellar restaurant I knew called Urban Angel, nestled in the cozy basement of a rowhouse in New Town. I ordered some greens and bread, far less traditional fare than I had for my breakfast, and looked down at the wood table where I sat, much like a farmers table with wide, light-colored boards. I ran my finger along the board seams while a small fire burned in the fireplace. I took out my Peter Pan notebook as I waited for my food. *Perfectly autumn*, I wrote on the page after I had written *orphan* before I wrote *bagpiper*.

I've had some firsthand knowledge of adoption in my life and the show took on even more meaning for me every time I remembered that Peter Pan and the Lost Boys (and Girls) lived as orphans. The orphan theme, be it in *Peter Pan*, *Harry Potter*, or our own life story, always reinforced the lesson of inclusion in this production. The experience of staging *Peter Pan* at Oakmont constantly reminded me that everyone wanted to belong, which increasingly put a greater strain on me to find a meaningful way for everyone to participate: sure, at times Karen had to cram dancers on stage, but my list of other participants kept growing: parents who wanted to help, enthusiastic students excited about seeing the ship, the members of our humanities committee, as well as our special guests from HOPE House, the Beacon of Hope, and the Friends Club. All these people responded to my invitation to play a role in the production, but it was left to me to effectively include them all, and I kept finding it a harder challenge than I expected. Adoption—and the process of bonding—is never easy, whether it's with one child or one hundred, and I often scratched my head trying my very best to accommodate each person—student, parent, and guest—in a meaningful way.

Act I, Scene 6: Kris

Good trip? Kris asked at our Monday 7:20 greeting.

Great trip. I feel energized, I said. *So many ideas, in fact—*

Here we go. What did you think of now?

A bagpiper.

The orchestration is written for harp, Jeff, pipes won't work.

In addition to the harp, I said.

There's no part written for bagpipe, I assure you.

Not in the pit, in the lobby.

It will be hard to hear in the auditorium.

Before the show.

Why?

Atmosphere. Barrie was Scottish. It'll make a rich experience.

Rich? How's the fundraising going?

Not that kind of rich.

Ok. Did Mr. Barrie play the bagpipes?

I don't know. I'm just going for a Scottish element.

A Scottish element? Kris raised his eyebrows and accented his voice on 'Scottish.'

Yes. Just for Saturday night. As guests arrive. Greeted by a bagpiper. In a kilt. I'll handle it.

You're going to wear a kilt?

No.

Thank God. You know, Jeff, Maine. That's all I'll say.
The bell rang.

I saw Frannie Conte in the school lobby in the pre-Thanksgiving bustle. Her daughter, Mia, was a senior and president of the drama club; I had known their good family for four years.

We can't wait for Peter Pan, Mr. A., Frannie said, smiling.

I'm glad, Mrs. Conte. I'm excited, too!

If you need anything—really, anything—please call.

I do need something, actually.

Anything, what?

I need someone to find a good price on a hotel room for the flying instructor. It's all we have to provide beyond the contract. Could you make some calls? Even if just over Christmas break

That's easy. Anything else?

Well, yes, actually. Your husband is a carpenter, right?

Yes.

Could he build a dog house? Teenager size?

I'm sure. Send me a picture. She giggled.

I wanted Nana's dog house to be a bit whimsical; not the proportioned sugar cube that most canines have in the back yard. Everything needed to be exaggerated: the door, the sides, and the roofline (which had to be strong enough for a flying Peter to land on). Mr. Conte captured it perfectly, and the kids painted it pink and white—perfect colors for a lady dog, despite that I eventually cast a senior boy, Aiden, in the role. No matter who or what I asked, families like the Contes always wanted to help bring *Peter Pan* to life.

That I spent the most American holiday in England watching Shakespeare didn't escape me—nor did the controversy I had stirred with the Nipmuc Nation, although I never heard from Chief Holley again. I remember in elementary school staging reenactments of the legendary First Thanksgiving with "Puritan hats" and "Indian headdresses" cut from colored paper. Before leaving, I delivered my pre-Thanksgiving lessons about the Mayflower Compact and Lincoln's proclamation as I had for many years, but—to Peter Pan's dismay—I again doubted myself. If I had so egregiously misunderstood this small cultural project with Mass Humanities, what did that say about my graduate work or my whole approach to history and teaching? I began the season confidently trying to address the problem of racial stereotyping and I felt I had failed despite my many hours of reading, thinking, and writing.

Plymouth, Massachusetts sits just ninety-eight miles from Oakmont. The scene from 1621 has worked its way into the American consciousness, with some fifty colonists sitting at tables and perhaps ninety Wampanoags reclining on the ground while the English shared their harvest. History, of course, makes a different case than the storybook: Wampanoag knowledge proved essential to English survival, knowledge that included not only agriculture, but also had its own understanding of government, philosophy, and culture—a culture predicated on giving thanks, especially for food. The celebrated peace between groups remained short-lived when King Philip's War erupted in 1675, irreversibly straining the Anglo-native relationship. While President Lincoln only officially declared the holiday as "Thanksgiving" during the Civil War, the sentiment has remained central to the American mythology, especially in the context of mutual sharing.[9]

Something even more insidious, however, surrounded the Native American discourse in the media stream that autumn.

Donald Trump's repeated bullying of Massachusetts Senator Elizabeth Warren, calling her "Pocahontas," angered me for two reasons: primarily for his overt racism, but also, Trump betrayed a complete lack of respect for the coequality of government branches. In spite of this anger, I thought the *Peter Pan* project would help, in some small way, challenge his hostility through dialogue, learning, and art. In *Pocahontas and the Powhatan Dilemma*, Rutgers University historian Camilla Townsend pointed out the distorted legacy of Pocahontas—who bore the name of Amonute. Townsend argued that the original fiction of a love affair between a young girl from the Pamunkey people of contemporary Virginia and the colonist John Smith flattered the dominant white culture—in some ways reinforced the idea of Montaigne's *bon sauvage*.

Pocahontas, as the scholarship demonstrates, worked hard to help her tribe rather than abandoned her people for all things English. Indeed, in the face of unstoppable European colonizers, Pocahontas and her peers "showed extreme courage and cleverness, sometimes even brilliance in the strategizing that they used.... [t]he most important lesson is that she was braver, stronger, and more interesting than the fictional Pocahontas," Townsend wrote. As with the Disney-fication of Peter Pan, the Pocahontas animated feature "conveyed more myths" than history, noted Townsend, but she continued by arguing that in the film, "the Native American character is the star—she's the main character and she's interesting, strong, and beautiful and so young Native Americans love to watch that movie."[10] Precisely for that reason—because both Barrie and Disney portray Tiger Lily as a simple, if not beautiful, sideline character, and because Donald Trump has weaponized the name of Pocahontas against a United States Senator—I wanted to be an influential part of a constructive process that, at least in these towns, reversed this insinuation and fostered a message of inclusion rather than exclusion. The early feedback I had received, however, suggested I misunderstood the issue as I waited for news from Mass Humanities.

The last week before any vacation can be a bit taxing: there's the appropriate adolescent excitement to balance against the teachers' own need for rest as well as their obligation to keep up with the curriculum. I tried to start Monday, December 18—the week before the holiday—focused to ensure for a smooth last week before the holiday break, until this email arrived: "Dear Jeffrey, It is a pleasure to inform you that a grant of $4,615 is awarded to you and Oakmont Regional High School in support of *Dialoguing with Indigenous Americans in our Community Through Peter Pan....*" Mass Humanities had agreed with our team and our educational vision for these students. Along with the four Cultural Council grants and two from AWFAE, funders both public and private invested heavily in this theatrical learning experience for Oakmont students, our diverse guests, and the wider community. As I felt the increasing weight of responsibility with the approaching new year, I always returned to the original objectives: to produce a familiar story to delight our community, to carefully include everyone who wanted to play a role, and grow—both individually and as an ensemble—in the scope of the endeavor.

Kris and I often throw at each other lines from Mel Brooks' movies. We're big fans, and the hour I spent with Mr. Brooks in 2018 at the Agua Caliente Resort in Rancho Mirage was one of the best of my life. One of my favorite lines, as said by the venerable Yogurt of *Spaceballs* is: "Merchandising, merchandising, where the real money from the movie is made." With a high school production, I only sought to meet expenses, not turn a profit. Yet, fish alone couldn't keep us in the black and I had another idea for holiday presents that I thought might sell. Steph's monochrome logo reproduced easily onto promotional items and I had it printed on spiral notebooks and pens with the phrase, "Today I will fly!" They were affordable, school-related gifts and I kept them a secret. Working with the school secretaries, I emailed the parents about the fundraiser, and I found some of "Santa's Helpers" to generously gift-wrap the sets before the holidays. On Christmas morning, 150 Oakmont students opened packages to discover that, along with Santa, Peter Pan had flown into our towns that night, too, with an encouraging message about their own ability to fly. For my teacher friends, I had lime-green ceramic mugs emblazoned with Steph's logo as Christmas presents, items that proved to be in great demand due to their finite supply. The mugs bore the motto "At Oakmont, we believe everyone can fly!" and reminded us with our morning coffee of our shared mission as educators. I also placed large banners with Steph's logo in the school lobby announcing Peter Pan's flight to Oakmont and, for the first time that anyone could remember, an unusual amount of interest in the musical buzzed around school as the clock struck midnight on a new year.

In the musical version of *Peter Pan*, intermission arrives not half-way, but two-thirds of the way through the production, after Peter's famous admonition to the audience to "clap if you believe in fairies." In the high school year, intermission arrives in January with semester exams. Unlike many colleges, however, the high school calendar reaches the midpoint of ninety school days after Christmas vacation, so when students return from their holidays in early January, they wrap-up first semester classes, complete projects, and write their exams in less than three weeks before starting a whole new slate of spring classes. January, then, is a time for new beginnings as students start a new schedule with new teachers, but also in the theatre program with auditions and new rehearsals; it's an unsettled time but, in 2018, we were ready to set sail on our journey to Neverland.

Good New Year's? Kris asked when we returned.

Pretty good. I took Jenn to Broadway.

Really? You bought Hamilton tickets?

Better. CATS. Second row. Rum Tum Tugger wagged his tail right in our faces.

Dear Lord, enough with the cats, Jeff.

It's eternal, Kris, like—

Good morning, Mrs. Champa, Kris interrupted as my friend Rachel made her way down the hall from the English department bearing a paper. *Your timing is perfect.*

Oh really? she asked, smiling. *I brought something for Jeff.* I read the name at the top of the paper she handed me: Sara, a quiet first-year student who participated in the fall Interclass Play Festival and who would audition for *Peter Pan*. Her words mesmerized me as I silently read the essay in the hallway:

"I take part in Drama Club," Sara wrote, "a wonderful community that has made a huge difference in my life. I've learned many things from my experience, such as how to laugh at myself when I make a mistake, balancing high school with this community, and how to be confident in front of a large group of my peers." After detailing some of her experiences, she concluded the paragraph by noting, "In general, I have become more confident in myself because of Drama Club, and everyone in this community supporting me. Overall, this great community has really helped me to learn and grow, which has boosted my confidence in the positive things in life." I asked Sara's mom if I could publish Sara's words in the *Peter Pan* playbill and she eagerly wanted to share Sara's words. In reading over her lines, a few words jump out at me now just as they did then: community, laugh, confidence, and grow. In just a single semester, Sara encountered what I worked so hard to infuse in the theatre program across all grades. Her words encouraged me to sustain the positivity I labored to foster in the community as auditions began. After a successful audition, I cast Sara as one of Tiger Lily's braves and, I'm happy to write, she has remained an enthusiastic club member.

I often said there's room for everyone on the Oakmont stage, and along with Kris and the team, I worked hard to ensure that. Our season typically began with an evening meeting for parents and students to discuss key dates, attendance expectations, and fundraising goals. I stressed that commitment exists at the heart of everything we do—it's a familiar message to the families of upperclassmen. Auditions would begin later that week with all students simultaneously on the stage to learn a few steps of choreography. While we find parts for all students, auditions help us match the best role for each of the talking performers. I still required an audition of all participants to bolster their confidence and form a team from the start: all students began the season on an equal-footing. I told the kids at the start of every year: I look for big, sparkling eyes, followed by a commitment to the cast. I also wanted students to help their peers, especially among the veteran actors; I highly valued those who supported the newer students with choreography, more than just showcased their own talent. Oakmont Theatre celebrates community, not celebrity. The initial challenge was always fitting sixty kids on stage to learn thirty-two audition steps. Karen, however, never appeared frazzled as she pushed up her sleeves and jumped into teaching; that year she introduced Hook's *Tango*. The cast's first steps that season began another masterclass with Karen Brown.

I needed to find a new choreographer for the school when I became director in 2015. A student, active in the robust Theatre at the Mount company at Mount Wachusett Community College (MWCC), mentioned Karen to me and then connected us, representing nothing short of a miracle. Karen earned glowing reviews from the students and colleagues to whom I spoke and I eagerly arranged to meet her and discuss collaboration. We both kept near-insane schedules, especially while she and her husband Ken built a new house in town. We scheduled a brief late-afternoon meeting at a local coffee shop, convenient as we each ran to our next appointment.

From the start, I found her full of energy, kind, and realistic. Karen's artistic vision for the future interested me much more than her resume of past productions. Given her abundant activity in neighboring school shows and at MWCC, she clearly produced solid work.

What do you think about a high school doing an old show like The Sound of Music? I asked.

It's sweet and classic, it works well for a high school.

How would you liven it up?

What do you mean?

Well, not nuns as Rockettes, but how do you make an old story relevant? I pressed.

It's in the emotion. The setting is a church or a garden, the dance is what expresses the underlying emotion.

I love that, Karen.

I'm pretty traditional, but I'm not afraid to break the fourth wall.

When she mentioned breaking the fourth wall, I knew I had found a collaborator. In *The Sound of Music*, her nuns appeared serene while the von Trapp children exuded limitless energy, providing a good start for us both with Oakmont Theatre. The following year, she wowed audiences by rocking *Grease*, complete with flips, twists, and lifts. I knew in tackling *Peter Pan* that this mom of three grown children would relish returning to the innocence of the Darling nursery and would help make these swashbuckling pirates far more funny than fearsome. When I asked her to reflect on the Neverland work, she echoed that idea as a brand-new grandmother. "Working on *Peter Pan*," she wrote to me, "fortified and reinforced my beliefs in always trying to find youth; I never let go of new and exciting adventures and possibilities, no matter how old I am. Without adventure in your life, you will simply grow up and fade away." Each year, when I would thank the adult staff at the closing curtain, I always said of Karen that she not only gives the students amazing steps to take, she more importantly gives them the confidence with which to put one foot forward—especially the boys. That, I think, remains her greatest contribution to Oakmont Theatre. Starting auditions every year with choreography, then, quite literally sets the stage for us as Karen's energy and passion envelop the kids. Despite understandable and unavoidable bumps along the way, we all strive to maintain that energy until the curtain falls four short months later.

We concluded the ensemble work with some group singing exercises led by Kris before hearing individual auditions. These less-than-five-minute performances provided an opportunity for the creative team—myself, Kris, and Karen—to consider specific students in specific roles. I typically asked students to learn a monologue and perform a memorized vocal selection backed by our accompanist, retired music teacher Sharon Sawtell. Working with these students year-round, Kris and I had a good sense of kids' abilities and vocal range, but the audition served as their moment to step into a character's shoes.

Two exceptional girls auditioned for the role of Peter and when the creative team convened to deliberate after auditions, we agreed—and I cast—the older Amanda as Peter and the younger Mary as the understudy. I write it that way because while I always assume full responsibility for the cast list, I solicit feedback from all the adults and we always reach consensus. While we hadn't assigned understudies in the past, the production of *Grease* almost derailed when Rizzo contracted debilitating laryngitis during production week (and thankfully performed flawlessly at the last minute). The extra cost and preparation dedicated to the flying effect presented too much risk to not cast an understudy for Peter. The girls would double; when one played Peter, the other appeared as Mrs. Darling and, given the months of work Mary would dedicate to the role of Peter, we agreed from the beginning that she would play Peter at the Saturday matinee. The choice amplified the strengths of everyone. A year later in *Evita*, I similarly split the role of Eva Peron between the younger Mary who played Eva Duarte of Act I, and the older Amanda played mature Eva Peron in Act II. The decisions surrounding Peter were unsurprising—wholly different from casting Mr. Smee and Captain Hook.

Max surprised me when he auditioned for the role of Mr. Smee. On the one hand, Max had already told me, or reminded me, that he was very involved in community theatre and he might not be available for *Peter Pan*. On the other hand, I also thought he might audition for Peter Pan himself when I made clear that vocal range—not gender—would determine Peter's casting. Max had conscientiously balanced rehearsals with his many afternoon commitments, both at school and in the community, and he clearly demonstrated his dedication to *Grease*; I knew he would do the same in *Peter Pan*. The role of Smee fit Max particularly well; it was entirely comedic, nonconformist, and less extensive than a leading part than Hook or Peter. When I asked Max a year after *Peter Pan* closed what single word Mr. Smee would use to describe our production of *Peter Pan* he said, after thinking for a while, "heights." Mr. Smee—in many ways the antidote to Captain Hook—feared heights in his bumbling humility and failed to believe he could fly like Peter and the children. Of course, we were also all trying to reach new heights through the experience of staging *Peter Pan*. As with many things Max says, the word stuck with me.

In other manifestations of the Neverland story, Smee appears as the jester, the comedic relief to sinister Hook. While he fulfilled this role, Max's representation of Smee gave me a greater affection for the "spectacled boatswain" of the *Jolly Roger*. In the character notes to the 1904 script, Barrie described Smee as "the only nonconformist in Hook's crew" at his introduction in Act II. As Hook's deputy, he also served as the Captain's only confidant; indeed, Barrie wrote that Smee was "always ready for a chat," but he also presented himself not terribly bright, having fallen for Peter's disguise towards the end of Act II. Barrie created a chatty, glasses-wearing pirate, seemingly unlike the others of the pirate band who listened faithfully to Hook's every word—not the easiest character to become, and yet, Max did. While I gave Max the widest space to create a silly Smee, I wish I had directed him to emphasize the nonconformity a bit more—I suspect he would have loved that. Max convincingly played the nonconformist Che in *Evita* the following year.

I did, however, ask Max to emphasize Smee as Hook's confidant, especially at the finale, and he got the mix just right. The crocodile, remember, eats Hook in the end; but, in our production Hook only fled from—rather than be devoured by—the reptile. In the very last moments of the show, as Peter and Jane sang the reprise to *Neverland*, I had every member of cast enter the auditorium: yes the adopted Lost Boys (and Girls), but also Tiger Lily and her nation, while the pirates—including Hook and Smee—scaled the ship. Why? Because everyone wants to see their kid included in the finale of a high school production, so I always stage a grand and truly inclusive finale. Hook, hat in hand and not consumed by the crocodile, sobbed on Smee's shoulder at that finale, standing away from the rest of the pirates who also in their simplicity, waved goodbye to Peter and Jane. Hook's own undoing became his isolation, not the crocodile's teeth. In staging that moment, however, affable Smee stood as the stronger of the two; emphasizing his role as confidant as well as nonconformist since no one else would dare comfort Hook, and Max beautifully sold it to the crowds.

Much more than Smee or even Peter Pan, Fred Rogers influenced my life in a profound way, as he did for millions of other American children in the 1970s and '80s. For years, students have commented on the similarity of my cardigans to his as I've tried not only to quote but also live, his belief that we are each special just the way we are. As a boy growing up off of Stowell Road in Ashburnham—like Max—one of the television moments I most vividly remember in Mr. Rogers' living room happened when he talked with Margaret Hamilton, the actress who immortalized the Wicked Witch of the West on screen. I imagine Idina Menzel of *Wicked* has become a more familiar witch to theatre students today; however, Mrs. Hamilton flew into our living room just once each year in the annual broadcast of *The Wizard of Oz*—she was THE witch of all witches. The episode re-ran on public television ten years after its 1975 debut, and I still remember Margaret Hamilton putting on her black dress and pointed hat while she explained make-believe to Mr. Rogers' television neighbors. The scene, still available on YouTube, stuck with me for more than thirty years and informed not only how I directed the pirates of Neverland, but also how I ask questions, listen, and encourage imagination in my classroom.

Since community sponsors generously funded the special children's performance, I wanted to avoid tears from scared tots in the audience. Oakmont pirates, then, wore brightly-colored Converse sneakers with their costume. They also played whimsical recorders as they danced instead of carrying scary daggers. To make sure they befriended their neighbors in the audience, Captain Hook's pirates distributed 400 eye patches to the kids at the show. On closing night, Max confessed that making a small first-grader smile at intermission became the height of his season.

As I introduced the Thursday night children's performance, with a nod to both my teacher—Mr. Rogers—and Margaret Hamilton, I brought Smee on stage with his hat in his hand. I first considered bringing out Hook, but I wanted to keep him a surprise. I told the kids that Max was just a boy in the tenth grade, that he did his homework like them, had a dog like them, was a brother like some of them, and wore sneakers like them. So although the music turned a bit scary when the pirates arrived, I reassured the kids that no one needed to fear any of the pirates—especially Max dressed as Mr. Smee. I consider that introduction of Mr. Smee the best artistic decision of my entire career, and its a memory I cherish today.

The biggest surprise of auditions, however, came from Captain Hook. Several strong male vocalists in the cast presented a few different options for the Captain, but I hadn't considered that a senior named James would audition as Hook—not for any particular reason, I just didn't expect it. He nailed his performance with a strong and expressive voice, bringing novelty to Hook as he had to the class clown Roger in *Grease*. James surprised me both as goofy Roger and sinister Hook; I knew him as a shy and affable student who excelled at playing trumpet and had a keen mind for history. Happily, I saw James develop a real fan club as he grew on stage.

In the 1991 movie *Hook*, Dustin Hoffman pointedly asked the rhetorical question: "what would the world be like without Captain Hook?" I repeatedly posed that question to the cast as James grew more confident in his delivery. At times, he almost stole the entire show from the Peters and I came to appreciate Hook the more I read about the villain. For Barrie, the Etonian elite—with its education and "dandy" manners—had lost its place in the new, industrial century. Indeed, in the original play, Hook climbed to his death "murmuring" *Floreat Etona*, "may Eton flourish." James Hook only found fame and power in Neverland where, like the Scottish Stuart kings, he ruled tenuously. Barrie described his appearance more than any other character in the stage notes:

> Cruelest jewel in that dark setting is HOOK himself, cadaverous and blackavised, his hair dressed in long curls which look like black candles about to melt, his eyes blue as the forget-me-not and of a profound insensibility, save when he claws, at which time a red spot appears in them. He has an iron hook instead of a right hand, and it is with this he claws. He is never more sinister than when he is most polite, and the elegance of his diction, the distinction of his demeanour, shows him one of a different class from his crew, a solitary among uncultured companions.... A man of indomitable courage, the only thing at which he flinches is the sight of his own blood, which is thick and of an unusual colour. At his public school they said of him that he 'bled yellow.' In dress he apes the dandiacal associated with Charles II, having heard it said in an earlier period of his career that he bore a strange resemblance to the ill-fated Stuarts.... Those, however, who have seen him in the flesh, which is an inadequate term for his earthly tenement, agree that the grimmest part of him is his iron claw.

Unlike the middle-class Darlings, Hook shows the benefits of a first-class education, particularly in speech: "Compare with them the children on this boat about to walk the plank.

Split my infinitives, but 'tis my hour of triumph!" but he could find no place in the new, modern world. Hook represented an elegy rather than a frightening nightmare which is why I think James, in all his personal kindness and compassion for others, excelled in the role.

Cyril Ritchard's portrayal of Captain Hook in the original 1954 Broadway production received great critical attention and represented a shift in the direction of the play to a more popular audience. Critics regarded Gerald du Maurier's 1904 Hook for his aristocratic "dandiness," in part to show the folly of the upper class to the new middle-class audience, an element missing from Ritchard's portrayal. Writing for *The New York Times*, Brooks Atkinson observed that the "superb" Ritchard appeared more clownlike and even burlesque than previous blood-thirsty captains: "There is nothing sinister about his Captain Hook, and that may be a blemish for playgoers who don't want traditions altered" (Oct. 31, 1954). American audiences appreciated the comedic Hook rather than the pitiable aristocratic Briton, while James found an equilibrium between the two personas at Oakmont.

Perhaps like Batman's Joker, Hook frightens us in his folly because in 2015 *Back Stage* listed the Captain on its list of "Fifteen Terrifying Musical Theater Villains," securing his place in musical theatre with Javert of *Les Misérables*, Mrs. Lovett of *Sweeney Todd*, and Macavity of *CATS*. Maurier's 1904 Hook would have unlikely made the list; but also, the list's currency illustrates the enduring popularity of this Hook for fifty years. Ritchard's character moved Barrie's aristocratic Captain to something more intriguing in his apparent madness which James also harnessed. By the end of the show, we pity Hook rather than fear him. "No little children love me," he confides to Mr. Smee. "I am told they [the Lost Boys] play at Peter Pan, and that the strongest always chooses to be Peter. They would rather be a Twin than Hook; they force the baby to be Hook. The baby! That is where the canker gnaws...." Hook's image endures not because we fear him like a wicked witch, but we sense—if not identify with—the loneliness under his anger, which James captured marvelously.

For the first time with *Peter Pan*, I invited boys in grades five through eight to audition for the role of little Michael Darling, a practice I continued and included girls in *Evita*. Three boys auditioned to be Michael, all of whom demonstrated clear commitment to the stage and their eagerness to be part of the production. While the youngest, Kaden, proved to be the most convincing Michael—especially costumed in pajamas and clutching his over-sized teddy bear—I decided to also invite the other two middle school boys to join the cast, one as a Lost Boy and one as a brave. Including younger students in the high school production widened the work of inclusion as well as generated enthusiasm and something of a feeder track for the high school program. Neither in *Peter Pan* nor in *Evita* did I regret the invitations I extended to the younger students.

Hook laughs at—rather than fears—Peter Pan; instead, Hook irrationally points his fear at the ticking crocodile. Fortunately for us, our costumer Doreen Croteau keeps an amazing crocodile costume in her wardrobe that uses a long skateboard to help the actor maneuver. Playing the crocodile on stage presented a great opportunity to many students, but especially for one apprehensive to sing and dance—and I had just the candidate. I smiled when Stephen joined the stage crew of *Grease* the year before, as I had when Mimi unexpectedly auditioned for the role of Cha-Cha. Stephen increasingly became involved with the Interclass Festival and I thought stage crew would be his entry into the musical, especially since many of his friends participated in the program. A talented athlete, Stephen ran competitively three seasons each school year, but I also knew him as a dedicated student, a sharp writer, and a good guy. I was thrilled when he told me he wanted to audition.

But for what role? I asked as we walked to the cafeteria.

I don't know. I pirate, I guess.

Give the audition your all, I think I have an idea.

From the start, Stephen *became* the crocodile—and he did especially well given his athleticism. The young children howled when he first crept on stage, his comedic timing was almost always perfect.

At his graduation party that spring, I asked him, as I had asked Mimi, to do me a favor before he headed to Emory University: to jot down a few notes about why, as a senior, he joined the musical. I've found these students, who first join during their senior year, often get the most out of each show, and they bring new energy to the production each season. Like Mimi, he began his essay with a caveat: "I will never be an actor, and my singing remains atrocious. Despite that fact, the musical became one of the most important things in my life. I loved the uniqueness of it—how different it was from everything else I had in my life. I loved how the musical united the school in a way that nothing else has," Stephen wrote. "I had never seen so many different kinds of people—actors, artists, engineers, musicians, teachers, dancers, and even an athlete or two—brought together in pursuit of a single goal. Even people from outside of the community contributed to making *Peter Pan* the best it could ever be." As a first-time actor, Stephen found and embraced the community that is Oakmont Theatre.

Like Stephen, not every kid wants to soar like Peter Pan or tango like Captain Hook; some contentedly join the ensemble to be among Tiger Lily's braves, the Lost Boys' family, or Hook's band of pirates. Kris, Karen, and I often emphasized that we found no small roles on the stage. We acknowledge members of the ensemble for being good helpers just as much as we work with the leads. Commitment, like inclusion, remains the paramount word for Oakmont Theatre. To ensure that everyone carries the same weight of responsibility in the production, I developed, after much discussion with Kris, rigorous attendance and fundraising policies that ensured everyone contributed equitably. In fact, one of my favorite scenes in *Peter Pan* included another group of students who generally didn't desire center stage but left the audience at peace: the lullaby animals of Neverland.

Doreen has almost every costume for every show imaginable, but not too many animal costumes beyond what's needed for *The Wizard of Oz.* I used to drive by one of her costume warehouse-workshops each day on my way to Starbucks, although I've been inside just once. The experience truly mesmerized me. Doreen remembers the smallest details from among the millions of items she has, from nuns' habits to Pink Ladies' jackets to Slovakian military uniforms. She costumed *Peter Pan* many times before, and ours was in many ways an easy job for her, except for the size of our cast.

I need the costumes for the lion, kangaroo, and ostrich, I said.

The what?

For the ballet scene. In act two. The animals, I said. Doreen never misses a detail, and I knew I confused her. She, after all, had helped stage *Peter Pan* far more times than I had.

Ballet scene? With the crocodile? she asked as we both started to laugh. I showed her the reference in my libretto. *I've never seen that done*, she said.

After the Lost Boys (and Girls) built a house for Wendy, and Peter set to guard it for the night, the animals of Neverland protect him as he falls to sleep; it's a sweet detail in the Broadway version that eases a part of Barrie's novel. The musical, like the novel, arranges the animals in a procession: "lions, tigers, bears, and the innumerable smaller savage things that flee from them, for every kind of beast, and, more particularly, all the man-eaters, live cheek by jowl on the favoured island. Their tongues are hanging out, they are hungry to-night" (68). In comparing the original *Peter and Wendy* to Robbins's musical, I usually prefer Barrie's tart moments to Jerome Robbins's saccharine, except here. The unspoken animal ballet became one of my favorite scenes in *Peter Pan*. The animals entered through the auditorium, gently distributing Pixie Stick candy to the children in the audience. Emma, who played the housemaid Liza, had an extensive background in dance and Karen choreographed a graceful ballet for her, creating the lullaby that put Peter to sleep. *The ballet scene*, Emma said, *was special because I incorporated something I've been working on since I was three onto the Oakmont stage, especially because I was able to portray the fluidity of dance as a message of friendship, which Peter Pan exemplifies.* Given Doreen's unfamiliarity with the scene, I surmised that many schools cut the scene, and I'm glad we did not. There are lots of special moments in the show, many of which include flying, but I'll always cherish those girls as gentle animals.

You look like hell, Kris said as we walked back from the auditorium after a long Friday rehearsal.

Thanks, friend. But you're right, I don't feel well.

Don't mention it. But seriously, are you resting?

Of course.

I mean, are you resting with your night job at the college?

Just doing what I need to do.

That's what I'm worried about, Jeff. The season is just starting.

I'm fine. Really, Kris.

Good. Because if you get any more white hair, nobody—and I mean nobody—is ever going to date you again.

And with that, my bestie turned right to head toward the band room while I walked toward my classroom with a grin. No matter how turbulent the flight to Neverland became, Kris always made it easier with his wit and his care for me. How lucky am I, and how lucky are his family and students, to have him as a mentor. But even his mentoring couldn't shield me from the heat I increasingly felt from the Humanities project and managing such a large endeavor with a part-time staff.

II

Part Two

In the second act, we fly to an island of fantasy, where we explore a forest with animals and a lagoon with a moored pirate ship.

Act II, Scene I: Dave

Admiral Lantry visited me during homeroom bearing rolled-up blueprints, just as the new semester began. He rarely ventured from the engineering shops to the back of the building near my classroom, so the visit brightened my day in the January gloom. *Plans for a ship, sir,* he said, unrolling them onto my wooden desk. *The starboard side of the Jolly Roger, sir.*

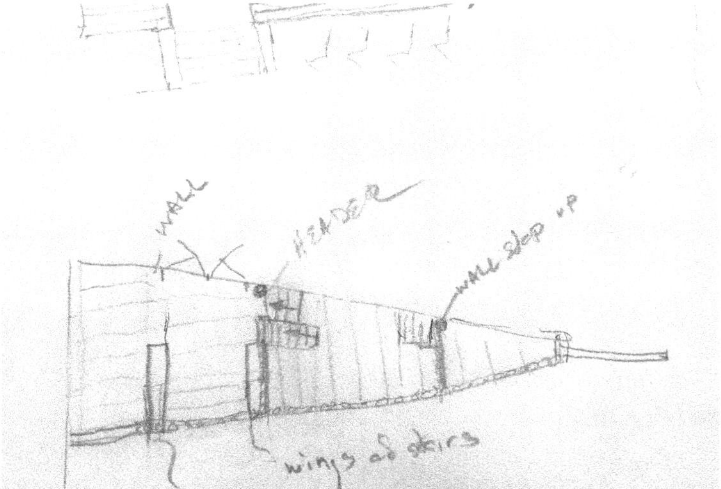

Original sketch of the Jolly Roger drawn by Dave Lantry.

Holy shit, Dave, I said, hoping the students didn't hear.

It will fill this entire wing space here, and we'll build a perfectly accessible fire escape through the hull.

That's so cool, Dave.

The quarterdeck will join the proscenium wall and the prow will extend right into the audience, stage left.

How far is that?

Thirty feet.

Crow's nest?

No, the Captain's deck is high enough, the masts and sails will extend right to the ceiling.

Stunned—even if by a police tazer—couldn't describe my feeling at that moment.

Now, serious question, he began. *Do you want portholes and is there a need for a plank?*

I do need a plank. Can I have portholes?

Of course. I also have three-inch thick hemp rope; we'll make it fire retardant and use it for rigging.

Will a plank be too much of a safety risk?

No, it will be retractable and hidden until needed.

How about a mermaid at the prow? I asked.

With clamshells?

No wait—how about a skeleton?

Skeletons don't wear clamshells, Jeff.

No, I know, Dave.

You figure that one out, I have a ship to build, he said rolling the plans.

I later re-read Barrie's own description of the *Jolly Roger*: "a rakish-looking craft foul to the hull, every beam in her detestable like ground strewn with mangled feathers. She was the cannibal of the seas, and scarce needed that watchful eye, for she floated immune in the horror of her name." As with Hook, however, there's humor beneath the frightening façade, as Barrie continued: "There was little sound, and none agreeable save the whir of the ship's sewing machine at which Smee sat, ever industrious and obliging, the essence of the commonplace, pathetic Smee" (166). Like Barrie's pirates, there's little to really fear in the *Jolly Roger*, although in scrutinizing Dave's plans, I feared the cost.

How much? I asked.

No idea.

Ballpark.

I need a thousand. No guarantees, you just pay the bills.

Of course. But who's going to build it?

My Materials and Construction class. They'll design it, select materials, and build as a class project.

That's brilliant, Dave.

It has to be fire retardant and that will cost. Everything has to be fireproof—nothing can burn.

We're good so long as it's behind the fire curtain.

But it's not going behind the fire curtain. It's going in the audience as a fixture. But don't worry.

Why?

I think Blessington Corporation in Gardner will donate the wood.

Really?

Yes. They do a lot with flame-retardant treated materials and I've been talking to them.

Wow. That's beautiful.

Make sure you send them a thank you.

Oh, of course, I said.

We're filling the auditorium with a ship, he explained, grinning, *to take us all to Neverland.*

Done, I said, shaking his hand as the homeroom bell rang.

Not yet. When do you need it?

April vacation the latest, a week before would be better.

Fine. But you keep everyone out of the auditorium D Block. We need to work in there.

I'll do my best, I'll talk to everyone in the office.

It must be secure so no one gets hurt during construction.

I understand, Dave. For all his dreaming, Admiral Lantry is always "Safety Davey," which is exactly why his career enjoyed such success. *Thank you, Dave. Really.*

Of course. We're family, he reminded me. He wasn't wrong. My sister Jenn had landed in one of his classes and he instantly became her favorite teacher in her twelve years of education in the school district. Dave attended her graduation party and I often ate at the Lantry dinner table. June and Dave included everyone and they always served as great role models at Oakmont. He wasn't building the ship for me, or even the show; he did the work for Oakmont—for the theatre, sure; but even more so for his students who will one day, when they are parents, mesmerize their own kids with a tale of building a thirty-foot pirate ship *inside* their school. *Peter Pan* inspired not only the cast as well as Kris and I, but others embraced the experience like Dave and Chris Wells in a new way. We all grew in new ways that spring.

I reached to pat Dave on the back as we parted: he walked down the hall and high-fived passing students who grunted "Lantry!" I turned left to go find Kris.

We have a ship, I said.

Great, I saw Dave walk into your room. How much?

He said at least a grand.

Ouch.

I'm going to use the lunch money we raised—especially from their fish fry. The connection is beautiful.

Good idea, said Kris.

Like Dave, my grandfather is a master craftsman. For a decade, including 2018, I lived just a mile from my grandfather and I regret I didn't visit him as often as I should. I love him, and he remains one of my greatest cheerleaders, but his independence and health keep him as busy as my schedule keeps me. As a boy, I spent much time with all four of my grandparents, each of whom shaped my life in significant ways. Like Peter Pan, not everyone enjoys the gift of grandparents; indeed, only my grandfather remained by the time of Peter Pan's visit. He's not as tall as me, but we share his white hair and blue eyes.

Despite not being as close as we were in my youth, our paths tend to connect each spring. He and my late grandmother loved musical theatre. He can probably sing every word to *Les Misérables* and whistle every melody in *Phantom of the Opera*. In fact, when Oakmont staged *Les Mis* in 2011, the spring before I returned there to teach, he went to the show. *I saw that in London and those kids did just as well as there*, he had said. He's come to all of our shows since 2016 and when I prepare for a production, he and I tend to visit more often. Perhaps as I approach 40 I still need encouragement from him. In the last few years, he's also generously shared his carpentry with the kids. I visited him one Sunday afternoon and we chatted for a bit about my parents in Vermont before turning to *Peter Pan.*

Boy, that car was something last year, he said remembering the full-sized Greased Lightnin' the Greasers wheeled on stage. *Got anything like that this year?*

Pirate ship. It's pretty cool.

Who made that?

The engineering teacher and his students. You should see it.

Nobody ever knows how many people work on a show like that. So much happens behind the scenes. Need anything else? he asked. My grandfather truly works behind the scenes, having counted just about all the money transactions at the parish church fairs, BINGOs, and most Sundays for the last half-century. Things happen because of him, and so few know it.

An old hand iron. Like this. It doesn't need to be detailed for the stage. I handed him a picture of an antique, but I wanted it lightweight for the housemaid, Liza, to pretend with.

Anything else?

This will bring you down memory lane, I said.

Yeah?

I took out another picture of a wooden dagger, crafted like a child's toy. *How many swords did you carve for us when we were small?* He has four grandsons.

Plenty, he laughed slightly. *None for Jenny or Carly.*

They've got to be exaggeratedly blunt so that everyone knows they're toys.

Dangerous times we live in.

No kidding. As blunt as possible.

I can do blunt. What color?

Green for the handle and metallic for the blade.

How many?

Two. And one last small detail? I asked. *I'd like to give them to the girls as souvenirs. Can you carve their initials into each as a keepsake? AP and MM.*

Ok. I'll take care of it.

He called two days later for a robust conversation.

Hi Jeff. Your order is ready for pickup.

Sounds good. I'll swing by on Saturday.

Ok.

Thank you.

Ok. Yup.

Click.

Spring teased us that Saturday as the remaining snow melted to reveal the sleeping grass.

Boy, it's nice out, he said as he opened the door—the same old, painted blue door I knew from childhood. I suppose few things remain unchanging in life, but for me, my grandfather has always lived in that small beige house with its blue door. He proudly reminds people that—not including his service in the South Pacific during the Korean War—he only moved once in his life when he bought his current house. *And I never had a mortgage; I used the GI Bill for that,* he told me once. The house on June Street is a small place; I can't imagine him and my grandmother there with four growing kids, but they managed. My grandmother passed away in 2003 and the house looks untouched: kettle on the stove for instant coffee, her still-life paintings on the walls, our school pictures scattered about (there's one of me before I got glasses in the fourth grade), with the same furniture in the living room and the same table and chairs in the kitchen. All that's different are the cookies in the jar and the newspaper crossword puzzle on the table—my grandfather's sharpened pencil and reading glasses still placed nearby. On that Saturday, however, an iron and two blunt daggers also sat on the table.

You went fancy on the iron, I said.

Just bent a piece of metal for the handle and layered some wood.

It looks authentic. You must remember those. The real ones, I mean. From the olden days.

He pretended not to hear me.

These ok? He picked up the identical daggers.

I traced my fingers over the initials: AP on one and MM on the other. Amanda and Mary had worked so hard to develop their roles, especially trying to give the other the creative space to create their own, unique Peter.

They're great. I said. *Really great. Thank you.*

Ok. What else?

You should come to look at the pirate ship. But come this week because the kids are about to put the clapboards on. You should see the steel skeleton underneath.

Ya? Steel, huh? Quite the project.

Can't burn, it's got to be fireproof.

That so. I don't know what Peter Pan is about. Never saw it. Mary Martin, right? Then Cathy Rigby?

You wouldn't believe how many people say that, I said. *And yes, you're right about those Peters.*

I could take a drive. What day?

Come Tuesday or Friday at 2:15. Call me when you arrive, I'll meet you in the parking lot.

Ok. I bet you're busy today, the show's not far off.

He was right; I had a million things to do, mostly shopping. *Thanks, Pep,* I said.

Ok. Take care, he said standing in the doorway as I walked to my Jeep.

See you this week at school.

We'll see.

I couldn't count the number of times I've driven away from that little beige house, first as a kid and then as a driver myself.

Every time I—and the rest of the family—drove away, my grandparents waited until we pulled out of the long driveway and turn onto June Street. He watched me that day, too.

My phone rang at 2:15 on Tuesday, but the call dropped as I stood in the middle of the cement-block school. The caller ID revealed my grandfather's number so I raced to the front of the school to find him. Not seeing him outside, I called back.

Hey, I'm at the front door, I said.

I'm out back by the football field.

Ok, stay there, I'll come to get you. I raced to the opposite side of the building, knowing that rehearsal would officially start at 2:20 but also that Kris would cover for me. I found my grandfather waiting by the backdoor in his green skiing jacket.

Cold out, he said.

Looks it. I've been inside since I got here.

What time do you get to work?

I try for 6:30.

He said nothing. Nor did he say anything when we walked into the auditorium and the kids gathered on stage. Disliking the silence, I jumped in.

So the prow is there, I pointed, *and the Captain's deck extends up there, all the way to the back wall.*

You can't block the stairs though.

I know, he's cutting a hole right through the side of the ship and the deck extends over the stairwell.

Wow.

He's rewiring the exit sign so that it's visible to the audience.

Holy smokes.

Look at the skeleton underneath the decks.

The steel skeleton of the Jolly Roger takes shape.

He shook his head, I assume in amazement.

It's about three times bigger than I expected, maybe four.

The kids did so much of the design and they're building it with the engineering teacher's help.

We built one when I was in trade school.

Really?

No. We just built shelves. For the library. They're still there. Built to last. He laughed.

Those shelves always remind me of the war. I laughed. *I mean the Civil War.*

Boy, this is something else. He ran his hand along the main deck. *All flameproof?*

Yes. Wait until it's finished.

It'll go quickly, I bet.

I hope so, we only have a few weeks left.

Wow, he said as we turned and walked back up the aisles towards the back of the auditorium. I don't remember talking as we walked towards the back door, but when I reached to open it he asked, *how will you top that next year? First the car, now the ship. What will you do?*

It's a big secret but I'll tell you. We're doing something different from Peter Pan. It's going to be Evita.

Evita, huh? I fell asleep at that. I think Mem was mad. Ok, we'll see ya, and he turned and walked into the cold alone to his car. I couldn't help but smile. Incidently, his contribution to *Evita* was refinishing a turn-of-the-century wooden wheelchair made by the Arrow Company of Erie, PA from which ailing Eva Peron made her final lament.

I later asked Dan, one of the sophomores in the Materials and Construction class that built the ship, about his first experience in theatre. I had the pleasure of teaching him in grades 9, 10, and 11, and I've seen him at work outside of the classroom. His interest in mechanics, robotics, and engineering has grown steadily across his high school years. He, more than any other student, worked extra hours with Dave to make the *Jolly Roger* perfect. "At the beginning of the semester, we had no idea where to even start the massive project, but over time Mr. Lantry's bold vision became more and more known to us until we knew exactly what to do," he wrote to me during his summer 2019 vacation. "From hanging roughly twenty feet above the auditorium floor to squeezing between steel struts in the underbelly of the ship, our crew transformed from simple 'wood techers' to proficient construction workers, a process I will never forget and will forever be proud to be a part of." By "wood techer" he meant a student in the Woodworking Technology class. Educators call this type of learning "authentic," in that the student solves self-identified problems and the learning becomes his or her own, as it did for Dan. The ship evolved from an idea, helped us meet the need for a set piece, and became a working laboratory—both for engineers and for actors—opening an entirely new window into the creative imagination of our flight school.

Dan adds the hull to the Jolly Roger.

Who were you with? Kris asked when I returned to rehearsal, breathless from running.

My grandfather.

I thought I remembered meeting him at Grease. He looked so closely at the work, I wondered if it was a building inspector or something.

Nope. Just gramps. What do you think of the ship? It's come a long way this week.

I'm wondering how many kids will fit.

Dave told me we can't go crazy.

Too late for you, Kris said.

Are the kids all warmed up? I asked.

They are, and ready to create.

Good, let's begin.

We have. Are you ready for the meeting, Jeff?

Which?

Thursday. For the project? Tiger Lily. What the hell do we call it?

The Humanities project. Yes, everyone confirmed. I have no idea how it will go. Better than the harp.

True, Kris confessed.

Should I ask Dave to build us a harp, as well as a ship? I asked.

Sure, but you still don't have anyone to play it, Tinker Bell.

Act II, Scene 2: Jeff

I proof-read, for probably the fifth time, the top of the paper I held in my hand as I stood over the copy machine. The presentation needed to be perfect:

Hearing Indigenous Voices in Our Towns with Peter Pan
A Project Funded by Mass Humanities
Agenda for Thursday, February 1 at 5:30 pm
Oakmont Regional High School
*** *** ***

Just copy it, I heard behind me in the teachers' workroom. *You're hogging the machine.*

It's got to be perfect, Kris.

And it is, will you relax and let me use the copier?

Ya, I said as I rubbed my temples.

What's wrong?

Another headache.

Did you take something?

Ya, it didn't help.

You better rest before 5:30, this has to be smooth tonight.

I know, Kris. Believe me, I know.

February 1 proved to be the real test of the Humanities project.

I chaired the meeting, but Kris, Dana, Cathy Stangroom, and four students also represented Oakmont. The four girls included: Mia as president of the Drama Club and whom I cast as Wendy, Amanda as vice president of the club and played the principal Peter, Eden as Tiger Lily, and Emma whom I cast as Liza the Housemaid but was also a student in my A.P. U.S. History class that spring. I asked Emma's mother, Kara Roche, a professor of English at nearby Mount Wachusett Community College, to provide her perspective as a parent, community member, and to help us tell our story through media outreach. Jim Eagle and Tammy Bucchino represented the local community and had already proved themselves enthusiastic collaborators for the work. Dr. Goodby and Dr. Stanley both confirmed their attendance early. Larry Spotted Crow Mann and Annawon Weeden had also confirmed, the former arrived with Cathy Stangroom—they appeared to be old friends, which reminded me that we all sought friendship around the table.

The Webber Conference Room sits across the hall from the auditorium; it's so close that the boys use it as their dressing room during productions. There's a long table in the middle, windows that overlook the school courtyard, and in the corners are piled boxes and other items lacking a permanent home somewhere around school. The room functions well for meetings, but it's hardly a board room. I set the table early with bottles of water and granola bars; a 5:30 meeting was atypical, but as some of our guests traveled long distances I didn't want to propose either 7:00 or 2:30 pm, and no one objected. The girls waited in the lobby to escort the guests to the conference room wearing their green and white Oakmont Theatre shirts, and welcomed our guests along the way. By 5:30 we had almost all assembled. I sat in the center and members from Oakmont and the communities sat at the two ends of the table while the guests congregated in the middle. Annawon had told me he would be late, but by 5:35 when Bob still had not arrived, I called the meeting to order. After introducing ourselves, we jumped right into the discussion: what to do about indigenous representation, especially the infantile "Ugg-a-Wugg" song? As we did not scribe the meeting, and only my notes remain, I won't try to recreate the dialogue here, but just make some broad points about the two-hour discussion.

First, the guests wanted to share their personal stories. Larry talked at length about how he desired to help us and gave us an overview of his work with social and public health. Jim Eagle related great stories about his father who, in order to be the breadwinner for their family, donned native regalia as a sideshow entertainer. Jim brought great personal insight to the intersection of culture and entertainment. Tammy saw the show as a teaching occasion, an opportunity to present the audience with artifacts and small vignettes about Native American heritage. Before the meeting, Tammy, Kris, and I had talked about an authentic drum circle—could we substitute an authentic drum circle for the "Ugg-a-Wugg" song? Tammy cautioned me about cost, but I considered anything. The conversation ranged widely, including discussions of regalia versus costumes, license and contract fidelity, as well as musical adaptations, until, about forty-five minutes into the dialogue, Bob Goodby arrived having mistakenly taken a wrong turn in our rural town. I was glad to have him at the table; his entrance gave me an opportunity to try to summarize our progress and how to move the conversation forward. I looked at Kris as I struggled to build consensus with this *ad hoc* group.

We all agree it's a problem, and we don't have any idea how to fix it, I said. Not long after this, Annawon entered as one of the girls then broke the ice.

Isn't it just a story? Can't we just tell the audience it's a story with good parts and bad parts?

Larry slowly nodded his head. *You're never going to successfully represent our culture,* he said.

We don't want you to represent our culture. Just like we don't want kids wearing feathers at Thanksgiving, Anawon added. *I don't send my daughter to school for things like that.*

Kara mentioned that the "Ugg-a-Wugg" dance from NBC Live (2106) energized that production. *Yes, they're silly words but it would be a shame to lose that energy,* she said.

Larry insisted we keep the show as written and explain that the story dated from another era.

Kris sat up in his chair. *Excuse me, sir, I just want to be clear: you're saying to leave it as written?*

I am, Larry responded.

Kris relaxed in his seat and we nodded to each other, knowing we had reached the breakthrough moment. The meeting had not at all gone as expected, but we began to find common ground and the shared vocabulary I had so desperately sought. Cathy offered some very good suggestions about wardrobe that could be consistent with the spirit of the work but was neither the buckskin of comic books nor actual regalia. We began to use the word "wardrobe" to avoid the extremes of regalia and costume. I looked at James Stanley and invited him to contribute more:

Stage it as it's written, it's an easy fix, he said. *You wouldn't be the first, but an explanation on stage and in the playbill would be a good gesture.*

Bob Goodby, like me, remained unconvinced. Yes, I wanted resolution, but I had thought about this problem for nine months and I felt the problem warranted more resolution than the ideas under discussion.

It needs a slap in the face, Bob said. *Something arresting. A show-stopper if you will.*

Could you please explain, Bob? I asked.

He agreed with what had been said around the table; we could never offer an authentic representation as Chief Holley had written in September. Furthermore, if we aimed to represent a Native American culture, which one would we choose? Barrie most likely imagined not the Nipmuc of Central Massachusetts but the peoples of the Great Plains, an area where we had no expertise to draw upon. I looked across the table at Dana, who always appears sensible, well-read, and has lived in Westminster almost his entire life.

It seems reasonable, but I don't grasp the show-stopper idea.

Bob envisioned doing the "Ugg-a-Wugg" song as written, with the comic book costumes and then, at the end of the song, having some sort of dramatic lighting effect that 'interrupted' the 'game' of the kids on stage. Then someone—maybe a member of the Native American community—could read a statement, explaining what Barrie got wrong but that the error didn't invalidate the good parts of the play, like the themes of loyalty and friendship. Additionally, we wouldn't really violate any terms of the licensing as much as push them; it would just be a mini intermission that rejected the status quo. We paused and each reflected before I broke the silence.

The action would send a clear message, I said. *We can perform the show as an historical artifact and then protest its message through interruption. I think the idea has merit.*

My niece Jasmine studies theatre at UMass, Larry said. *She could help you. I'll send her information tomorrow after I speak to her.*

Thank you, I said. I hadn't been so grateful in months. *I believe we have a starting point.*

We all nodded. The committee left the details to me and the creative team to sort out, but we had reached a consensus: do the play exactly as written, and learn from Barrie's—and Jerome Robbins's—time-bound mistakes. We agreed to meet at a rehearsal in a few weeks to review the progress. At adjournment, I saw only handshakes and smiles. We had built a bridge, but before everyone left I had one question: *What about the tipi I bought from the Crow Nation for Tiger Lily? It's coming all the way from Montana.*

Use it, Annawon said. *We're not Crow, we won't be insulted.* He smiled. *And I don't imagine they would be either; I bet they were happy to sell it to you.*

As I prepared for bed, my sister asked about the meeting:

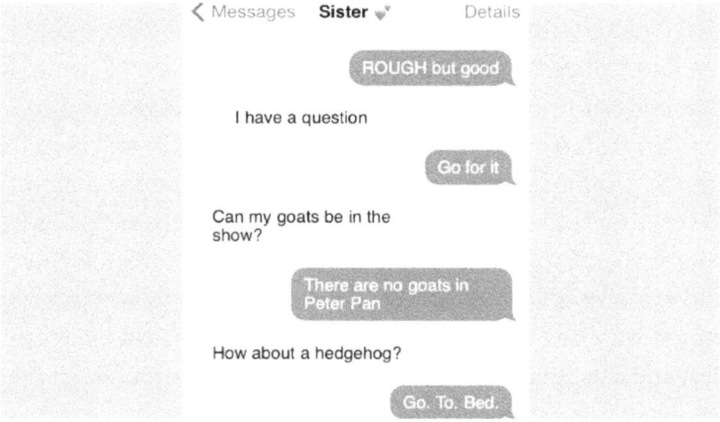

Our morning hallway chat focused on the previous evening's

work.

Well, are you pleased? Kris asked.

I'm exhausted and I'm very relieved. What did you think, Dana?

I thought we were headed for disaster, but we found traction and I think we're now on firm ground.

I agree, Kris said. *Do you know how you will stop the show?*

I could try an on-the-spot heart attack.

At four performances though?

Dana laughed.

I really don't know, Kris. I'm going to reach out to Jasmine and talk to her. She may well be the key to all of this.

Don't wait too long, you've got to get this squared and get the story out before someone else does, Dana said with Kris nodding. The bell rang and we dispersed to our classes.

Kara got to work on helping us tell our story. We walked a fine line in maintaining fidelity to the licensing contract and acknowledging the inappropriateness of the *Ugg-a-Wugg* scene. Kara started her press release with a great hook, inviting readers to "four performances of *Peter Pan* like you've never quite seen it before. They never doubted they could fly, and you're about to see why." She continued to explain the focus of the Mass Humanities work to tackle, head-on, the racial stereotyping in the play, "What has been created, through honest dialogue with local experts and scholars in Native American heritage, is a unique, artistic vision, visually poignant and stunning, where the *Peter Pan* we all know, love and remember is kept intact, but where stereotypes are no longer honored or accepted." She later confessed by email that she was skeptical of the work, but after the meeting, she "realized it is never wrong (or too late or too daunting or too silly or too hard) to care about doing what is right, *not* what is popular." The local newspaper, *The Gardner News*, ran the story "Reinventing Peter Pan" on April 17, 2018, and through their combined words, Kara and Doneen Durling of the local paper also helped us reach a new height of success.

A week later, the student leaders of Oakmont Regional gathered after school without knowing why. The combined groups included members of the Student Council, National Honor Society, Peer Leaders, and Students Against Destructive Decisions. Sixty students filled the cafeteria and I arranged them at the tables by grade, rather than by club, with snacks. I also had class lists, "never grow up" pens, and 800 Valentines:

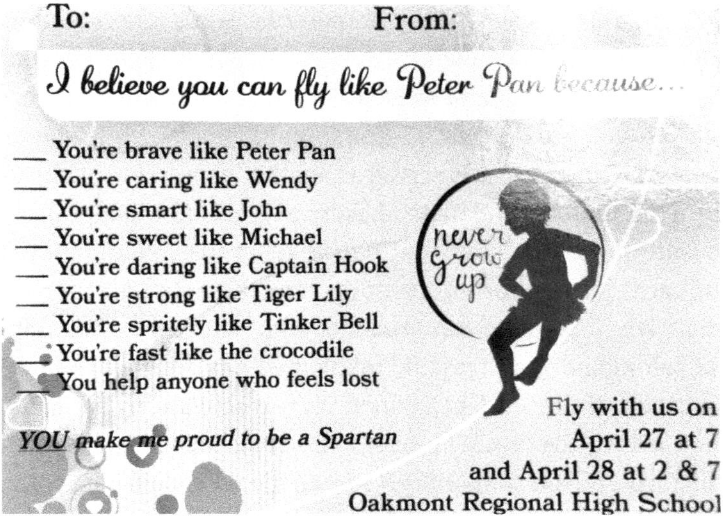

On the reverse, I printed the service organizations' logos and a quotation so important to the Oakmont community that the faculty stenciled it on the walls of the library: "On this day, choose joy, choose hope, choose life, choose love...and they are yours." Mr. Tom Anderson, Oakmont Librarian from 1996-2011—whose work I continued in the library when he became ill—penned those words in his decline. The statement reminded us of his legacy—less of books and research, and more of kindness and love—the message I wanted to share both with *Peter Pan* and on Valentine's Day.

With the help of the groups' advisors, I asked the student leaders to personalize one card for each of the 780 Oakmont students and teachers, focusing on their grade-level peers. Brittany Smeltekop and the members of the Friends Club worked in their monthly meeting to inscribe the cards for their club. I encouraged all the students to write them for their friends and ensured that no one was left out. The students then organized the cards by homeroom, triple-checked the lists, and student councilors delivered them on February 14. Every Oakmont student received a message of affirmation that year on Valentine's Day. Some found it hokey while some relished it, but the cards served as another expression of unity from the students and their advisors who brought that project to fulfillment. The Student Council generously paid to have the cards printed for the event to show their support for the initiative. "Some of our students who sometimes feel left out felt included and joyful," explained Advisor Dan Dufour on behalf of the Student Council. "I was still seeing some of the cards tucked away I binders and book bags in May, so it must have meant something." Just as the notebooks that read "Today I will fly!" reminded Oakmont students that the adults in their life believed in each of them, the Valentine's cards also reminded them their peers believed in them as well—just like Mr. Anderson had.

National Honor Society students prepare Valentines.

The Valentines continued to build springtime enthusiasm for *Peter Pan* with a bit of sweetness, but the project didn't get us anywhere closer to producing the show. We rehearsed with Sharon at the piano every Tuesday and Friday from 2:20 until 5:00, with the days chosen to avoid conflict with standing appoints in the music program. Just as the athletic teams have coaches and assistant coaches, it takes—in addition to the accompanist and director—the music teacher and the choreographer for us to effectively rehearse. Unlike a sports team, however, I did not call every student for each rehearsal and I diligently scheduled specific scenes as early as December so that students and their parents could best manage their schedule, since each actor committed about fifty hours of rehearsal before production week began.

We started rehearsal with announcements and I shared a motivational idea with the cast. Kris and Sharon would warm up the students' voices with some exercises after which we reviewed the work of the last rehearsal before jumping into a new scene or dance. The adults of the creative team worked collaboratively; for example, Abigail, who is as talented a pianist as she is an actor, told me that "the way you and Mr. DeMoura interact makes rehearsals more lighthearted and fun, and I think it leads to so much creativity because you're both so devoted to what you do." I often asked Karen to help the kids cross the stage without appearing awkward. Kris questioned anything on stage he finds out of place, and he often asked me which orchestral sounds I want more or less of. I couldn't help teenagers create something as complex as a Broadway show without the help of such talented collaborators.

In addition to learning their lines, the kids had to do a fair amount of imagining until April before any sets were built or the costumes arrived, and they demonstrated great flexibility when the carpenters built the set larger—or smaller—than they imagined, or their costume fit differently than they expected. In all, it represented about a sixteen-week season that culminated in just four performances in a single weekend.

During production week, parents and colleagues used to all uniformly say "you'll be so glad when it's over next week." They learned that isn't true. In fact, the week following the production was often the hardest of my year. While the focus of my work occurs in the spring, I would announce the next year's show at the closing curtain and, like *Peter Pan*, each show became an eighteen-month—rather than annual—cycle. Just as some mothers struggle with depression after a nine-month pregnancy, sometimes the let down from my eighteen-month work could be hard. Thankfully, my friends cared for me in the days following a show.

Karen taught night classes at area dance studios when she wasn't helping with our show. As a result, she couldn't attend the Humanities project meeting. I could tell she felt uneasy with my "show stopper" explanation.

It will throw off the kids, throw off the show, she said to me privately after rehearsal.

I hear you Karen, but with all this project's work, and the seriousness of the racism, we have to do something.

I agree, I agree, I just wish it wasn't that. Think about flow.

I'll do my best to find the right solution, Karen.

Of course you will, she said, reinforcing her support.

Karen is always a good sailor. She never hesitates to share her good opinions, but also doesn't rock the proverbial boat. She confessed her frustration to me, but I also had to balance that frustration with the project goals. I also consider her a close friend and I empathized with her frustration. The kids shared her anxiety about this unknown "show stopper." After Kris, Karen has always been my most supportive lieutenant and I didn't want to anger her as I increasingly saw that this would. I kept making a mess even messier.

Kris also approached me that afternoon about a schedule conflict. March is traditionally "Music in Our Schools" month and several K-12 concerts utilize the auditorium, which is a big reason why we couldn't construct sets earlier than April. The ship stood in the way of some temporary seating for the very popular concerts. I couldn't, however, slow down Dave and the engineering students as I feared they'd miss their deadline. While Dave, Kris, and I are the best of friends, conflicting priorities that spring heightened the tension among us. For all my talk of inclusion and Valentine's cards, I feared that resentment crept into the project, despite everyone's best effort. None of us ever lost our cool, but the strain shortened my temper and I began to crack. Mr. Uminski stopped me in the hall one morning and asked if all was well.

I'm fine. The show is fine, I said, maybe even grunted.

I'm sure, just make sure you rest over February break, ok?

I needed a vacation to another far-off place. Like Peter Pan, I often need to escape to adventure and even a bit of danger.

Jasmine took a few days to respond to my email and then, when comparing our calendars, between her spring break and my February break as well as her own show, we agreed to meet on March 24. Although this date fell later than we anticipated, it was the only date we could find. I had no doubt she would keep the appointment, and to make it easy on her, I agreed to meet her at the Starbucks in Amherst, Massachusetts, giving me time to ponder this "show stopper" business before I pitched it to her. I still searched for the best option for the kids, even though I didn't really know for what I was searching.

Act II, Scene 3: John

The period leading up to February vacation included many starts and interruptions, not the least of which was the beginning of the new semester at the end of January. February vacation, in some ways, felt like another interruption; however, the time away refreshed the kids so that we returned ready to fly through April. I usually didn't schedule rehearsals during February break and Kris and I would each try to go away at least for part of the week to also refocus, especially that year. In 2018, Kris and his wife Jenn, along with their son Creighton and daughter Kielyn, unexpectedly drove south to Florida to visit Kris's parents—a choice that made me happy because Kris's father had been ailing with Parkinson's disease. The last-minute and surprise nature of the trip made it fun and I felt happy for them. In January, I invited John to London for a weekend never thinking he would agree—and he stunned me when he did. While our friendship had, in the months since *Grease*, enjoyed something of a renaissance—we met in Cambridge when he visited Boston that June, and I returned to California in August—we hadn't been together since summer.

John flew directly from Los Angeles to arrive a day early and tackle his jet lag. Waiting for my evening flight in Boston that Friday, he sent a video of him singing "Feed the Birds" from *Mary Poppins* outside of St. Paul's cathedral. The movie held an important place in his childhood, and he once credited singing along with the film as the start of his music career. I wanted to share his happiness when I arrived the next morning. He looked tired when we hugged at Victoria Station twelve hours later—the sort of hug with which old friends greet each other. Since I had business in the city, he took my luggage and returned to his room while I headed off with my leather knapsack. We planned to meet at the hotel that afternoon.

Several families in the community adopted me during my eight years at Oakmont. I especially felt adopted each June when families invited me to graduation parties. With some families, however, those invitations extended year-round and have sometimes endured long after the student graduated, as was the case with Chuck and Megan Reitz. Their daughter Mimi worked as an *au pair* in Paris that year and the distance weighed heavily on both her and her parents, so when I arranged my London trip, I asked Mimi and her parents if she would like to eat lunch in London. Mimi caught the train and returned to Paris in time to put her charges—Jean and Salome—into bed.

So Mary Poppins, how are Jane and Michael? I asked her as we walked past Buckingham Palace and toward the Churchill War Rooms. I had visited the Reitz family on Christmas Eve, and heard most of the events of her adventure up to that point. Although Mimi and my sister weren't friends in school, they graduated only a year apart; in many ways, our three-hour London tour reminded me of my time there with Jenn the year before.

It's Jean, not Jane, and Salome, ils sont français.

Mary Poppins was a nanny, her kids were Jane and Michael.

Jeff!

Westminster Abbey, there, I pointed as I taught along our walk.

Kate and Wills, she beamed. *I got up early with mom that day to watch the wedding on tv.*

Parliament just there. Peter P—

I know, I know. He jumps on the clock. Enough with Peter Pan, she snapped before giving me a smile.

After touring Churchill's underground bunker and a warren of war-time offices, we headed north toward the British Museum, exchanging the legacy of World War II for the ancient Elgin marbles. Nearing twenty years-old, Mimi had gained much confidence through her overseas work and, while I had protested strongly against the idea of a gap year, her success in Paris had proved me wrong. That afternoon, I burst with pride for her while feeling the fatigue of the transatlantic flight.

At Trafalgar Square, we patted the bronze lions and looked down Whitehall at the clock.

The Lions. They remind me of CATS, I said.

Jeff. Too much CATS. It's a weird show, except for the dancing. Don't take Mr. DeMoura's side.

Ok, ok, how's the HOPE House project coming?

Really great. We raised all the money and the NHS kids paid for the bus. It's all set.

That's great Jeff. She looked down, probably at a pigeon.

I wish you could come. It was all your idea, Mimi.

Jeff. It's an ocean away. I'm not coming home just for a weekend.

I looked at her but said nothing.

Ya, but, you're crazy to come here for the weekend with John. You should have just gone to L.A.

Same distance.

I know the show is important to you, it's just not in my budget, Jeff. I'm a poor au pair. *I'm sorry.*

I understand, of course. It's a silly show, I said as I nodded in agreement.

It's not silly, she continued, *but going home for it is excessive. So what are these marbles we're seeing?*

We said *au revoir* at St. Pancras Station; with Mimi headed to Paris and me to Victoria Station. *The show will be great, Jeff,* she said hugging me. *Make those kids fly, the HOPE kids will love it.*

I pulled a book wrapped in brown paper from my knapsack and handed it to her.

Merci. What is it?

Open it on the train. See you at home this summer. Be great!

With that, she headed through security and I dashed to catch the tube. When I emerged from the underground to find cell service, I downloaded a smiley text message from Mimi. I responded as I stepped into the lobby of the Grosvenor Hotel: "To read to Jane & Michael."

I had left her with a French copy of *Peter Pan dans les jardins de Kensington.*

John and I each had a room at the grand old hotel conveniently located above Victoria Station. When I checked in, I found my room on the top floor, up in the eaves. The Grosvenor was the first London hotel to install a lift—and for good reason. When I caught my breath, I texted John and he brought up my bag.

You're like the Hunchback up here, he said as I opened the door. *Or a consumptive seamstress named Mimi?*

Hello, old friend, I said as we started to laugh.

This moment felt less rushed than our earlier greeting.

Meet in the lounge in an hour? he asked. *Before the show? You can tell me all about your adventure today.*

Sounds great. I'll meet you downstairs.

Six months had passed since I last saw John and, while we text on most days, we almost never talk at length on the phone. Much like the previous April at his Beverly Hills gig, the first drink of the night passed with some awkwardness and perfunctory updates. The clumsiness of the conversation subsided when we took on London like we were 20. We splurged in every possible way that weekend; for the first time that we could remember, we both found ourselves simultaneously single and somewhat carefree. I asked John to choose a show for the evening and, while I'm always a sucker for *Phantom* in London, he wanted to feel the toe-tapping sensation of *42nd Street*—and I indulged with second-row seats. The magic of that night, however, happened over pizza at a delightful place in Neal's Yard called Home Slice. I asked for red wine when we sat down to a rustic table made of light-colored boards.

The same, he echoed.

Make it a carafe, please. I said to the waitress. I remember little more of that discussion except for our many laughs—the kind of laughs that only best friends ever share. Peter Pan's absence that night felt refreshing.

Everything sounded very loud the next morning when I found John in the breakfast room, but I resolved to keep pace with him. I needed a brisk walk after my full English breakfast and our first stop became Kensington Gardens. The February air cooled my face as we walked along the Serpentine, a walk I first took with my ex-wife in 2004 and had taken the previous December with Jenn, and the day before with Mimi. Whenever I'm in London I try to escape the city for a bit and find Frampton's bronze statue of Peter Pan in that little marsh where Peter's pram turned over. The inlet with its ducks has become a place that I've shared with the most special people in my life.

Unfortunate circumstances surrounded the 2004 trip. Our daughter Arabella was born still that May. While my ex-wife thankfully recovered quickly from the loss, that summer proved a dark time for me, and I turned to read *Peter Pan*—perhaps in an attempt to reclaim the innocence and security of the nursery. So my journey with Peter Pan started in the heat of that summer, in the green New Hampshire countryside, and when we needed a break from the grief, we embarked on a journey to London—and Kensington Gardens—our first trip as a married couple. The whimsy of the Frampton statue, along with my reading of the book, has since happily tied Peter Pan to my daughter. John knew this back story and the rich significance of standing at the statue wasn't lost on him. After the years when John and I lost contact, he gave me that old copy of *Peter and Wendy* knowing well what it meant to me.

There he is, I said, taking my hand from my pocket to point.

Charming. Really, it is. The water and the birds and everything makes it so lovely.

I like how all different people enjoy it here—runners, tourists, families, and friends.

It's sweet, he nodded. We watched the people pass by, breathing in the winter air.

Peter Pan from the Franpton bronze, Kensington Gardens.

The Frampton bronze manifests the whimsy of Peter in the soft, slender lines of late childhood; this piping Peter is neither wholly boy nor grown man as he plays. Around the base of the statue gather the animals, nymphs, and Wendy whom he summons with his playing. When I first saw it in 2004, I innocently imagined in my grief my daughter playing among them. Frampton's Peter, however, captures a slight masculinity that the female-cast Peters—first Nina Boucicault, more recently Mary Martin and Cathy Rigby—mask. The Broadway and Disney renderings of *Peter Pan* have made Peter much more impish than boyish. In his 1954 review for *The New York Times*, Brooks Atkinson wrote that Mary Martin "radiates...humor and delight," the portrait of Peter we have all come to expect. While I followed convention and cast girls as Peter and his understudy, I directed them to amplify their teenage frustration more than whimsy. Perhaps the most famous line of the original story—omitted by both Broadway and Disney—is Peter's claim in Act III that "to die will be an awfully great adventure," presenting a dark contrast to his command to "think lovely thoughts." Frampton's work entertains both extremes of Peter's character. After the Darlings adopt the Lost Boys (and Girls), we grieve for, rather than emulate, lonely Peter in his Neverland. Even in the statue he calls his friends to him, but they remain distant.

One of the great traditions in Oakmont Theatre has been to gather as a club after some late-season Friday rehearsal for pizza and to watch the film version of the show. Rather than screen one of the many cinematic interpretations of *Peter Pan*, I played *Finding Neverland* which so sweetly blends the play's fiction with episodes from Barrie's life, helping students to know more of the playwright's persona than what we glean from *Peter Pan*. The film portrays Barrie's care for the Llewelyn Davies family well and makes clear that Barrie himself didn't escape to the fantasy of Neverland, but instead embraced the mantle of caretaker for many. Similarly, folklorist Jack Zipes described Peter not as an escapist perpetual child as much as "a rebel who consciously rejects the role of adulthood in conventional society," a society as he points out, structured by both imperialism and industrialization, which makes the work almost serious. Standing in bronze in the Gardens, Peter taunts us in his freedom in Neverland—representing a trade-off between liberty and companionship, something that frustrates most teenage boys.

He's almost sad, I said.

You think? John added.

Almost. Maybe lonely. He just doesn't fit in. I think lots of kids feel that way, don't you?

Come on, let's get some coffee, John said, whisking me away toward the Italian Gardens.

I want to get the kids something special for the show, I said turning to him as we walked.

Like what?

Kris gives the seniors in band and chorus a flower at the final concert of the school year. I did that for all the kids in Grease, but I want it to be something special this year. He listened and looked straight ahead, his nose red from the chilly air. *I want it to be something they'll never get again in their life.* I stopped walking. *Will you write a song for them, please?*

A song? About what? he asked as we resumed walking.

Neverland. And never growing up. And friendship and belonging.

We walked on, searching for Pret a Manger with Peter piping to our backs. John only smiled.

We stopped for brunch at Fortnum's as we meandered through

the city, popping into a pub named The Mad Hatter—significant because John once played the Johnny Depp version of that character on stage—and wound our way toward the Thames. We were good friends walking and talking at our leisure.

What makes you tick? I asked. *What do you want in life?*

Four walls and room for a piano, he fired back without pause.

Huh? Four walls?

I always have an apartment. I want a house where I can make music without complaints from the neighbors. A house in L.A. isn't happening soon.

We laughed.

Clever, I said. *Four walls and a piano. I didn't know you were such a homebody.*

We walked along South Bank, retracing the steps where I showed my sister Peter Pan flying across the clock face, and pulled ourselves up to a table, again made of rough-hewn lengths of light-colored wood, in The Swan—the idyllic tavern adjacent to Shakepeare's reconstructed Globe theatre. John faced north and saw the river and St. Paul's cathedral illuminated through the windows while my view looked down the hallway at the loo. Darkness came, along with the stars to Neverland.

Tell me more about this song, he said.

I'd pay you. My own money. It's my gift to the kids.

Tell me about the song. He emphasized "song."

It's just an idea, really.

I like your ideas, let's hear it.

Peter doesn't fit in, like the Lost Boys, but they're family—sort of like the cast, I suppose. Orphans.

Orphans?

Did you ever think of that? Peter Pan and the Lost Boys are all orphans. Like Harry Potter. Or Dorothy. Or Mowgli from The Jungle Book.

You must miss India with all this thinking of London, John said.

I am ready to return to the exotic, I said, sipping from my drink.

I guess orphans do want to belong, John said.

Yes, they do. Despite Peter's protest.

It's not the thing I usually compose, Jeff.

Melodically it is, I can imagine Faultlines playing it. The subject is different though.

I do need a new project.

You'd have to sing it to them, though. After the show. That would be part of the deal.

Weekends are hard, that's when I have gigs.

I know. I'm not looking for free. In the silence, I ran my finger along the gap in the boards.

St. Paul's is pretty in the light, he said. *We've bookended the day—first with Peter Pan for you and now Mary Poppins for me.*

Our eyes met and we smiled before I returned to stare at the wood tabletop. I didn't push the song any farther, but later that night, I looked at him—right in the eyes, a moment I'll never forget—and was wholly honest, with both him and myself. *I need you to come to Peter Pan, John. I know it's a silly show, and it's far away from California, and it's a pain to come east, but for whatever reason, this has become important to me, and I can't imagine you not being there. I'm not even talking about the song.*

He exhaled and shrugged his shoulders slightly. I've learned that while John can be slow to decide sometimes, he never agrees to something he won't do. *I know*, he whispered. *I'll go. Of course I will.*

Neither the Brothers Grimm nor Walt Disney scripted our airport goodbye the next morning. Like Cinderella, we stayed out too late; and unlike her, for us, it was long past midnight. Our friendship existed so often in the extreme and I surmised on the flight home that while we had enjoyed many soaring heights that weekend, we might resume a period of silence in the months that followed. I felt crushed and deflated. I wanted the extraordinary to become typical, but we both had to return to the ordinary. He texted to say he made it home safely, but little else. John retreated again; I returned to work feeling sad and lonely.

The first rehearsal after vacation didn't go so well. I longed for London and our carefree weekend. John and I had never spent that much time together and the subsequent disappointment hurt. I walked as if in a fog and my patience had worn thin.

Great news, Kris said as we finished rehearsal. *I found a harp.*

I raised an eyebrow and looked at him: *Really?*

No, but you're in such a pissy mood I thought I'd try.

I cracked a smile.

How come you're so blue? he asked.

Dunno. Hard for me to come back sometimes.

Well pick yourself up, you've got to get these kids in the air.

I know. How's mom and dad? I asked.

Good. It was great to see them. Dad looks tired but we had fun. And I got my family to Disney.

I'm so glad, Kris. Really.

Did you get your bagpiper?

I was in England, Kris, not Scotland.

You're telling me there's not a bagpiper in all of London? I'm pretty sure the Queen has one handy.

Ha. Do you have the palace phone number?
No, but really, did you find one?
As a matter of fact, I did book a piper, more locally.
Good. Ask him if he has a harpist cousin.
Ha. Ok.
Make sure he lives nearby, we can't reimburse travel.

Two days later, I received a text from John:

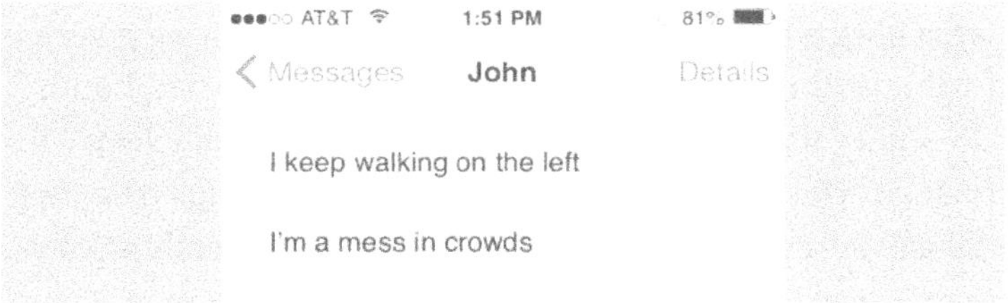

I didn't push John about the show or the song. I had new confidence once John texted and soon enough I found other show headaches to resolve. Although tickets didn't go on sale for five weeks, parents began worrying about a scarcity of seats. Tickets became an April problem that suddenly consumed my February. I replied to John as if nothing had happened. I vented to him about the tickets, knowing Kris didn't need to hear any more of my complaints.

Act II, Scene 4: Kris

March blustered through as we exchanged the February weeks of calm sailing for, as Admiral Lantry said, the "all hands" call—quite literally as his students built their *Jolly Roger* in dry dock. The phrase, "mad as a March hare" rings true, not because we're rabbits invading the school like Watership Down, but the pace of spring in school always felt slightly mad. Time, however, isn't always so frenetic. As Mr. Smee admonished Captain Hook: "Someday, the clock will run down, and then the crocodile will get you" (73). And so it will for us, in so many ways.

Kris is my closest friend at Oakmont, which is not surprising given our shared interests and how closely we have worked together. Yet, I also developed a close friendship in the last few years with my classroom neighbor, Dana Altobelli. Dana joined the Oakmont faculty as a new teacher when I was a student in the 1990s, but I didn't know him then. We became friendly when I returned to Oakmont, but not extraordinarily close; however, we developed a close mentorship when Mr. Uminski assigned me to teach in the classroom next to his. The timing also coincided when I cast his son, Stephen, as the crocodile. I learned that Dana's generosity overflows when he shares his time and energy. *Whatever you need me to do,* he said when Stephen started rehearsals, *just let me know.* Dana has talents far greater than selling concessions or ushering, especially as an outdoorsman. As an historian, I asked him to sit on the Humanities project committee, with whom he shared many ideas, but I knew his talent remained untapped.

The tipi is finished, I told him one morning in the corridor. *It's shipping from Montana.*

Excellent. Like Annawon said, it's good that you're going authentic and supporting artisans, he reasoned.

Shipping tipi poles from Montana isn't cheap, though. I said as he raised an eyebrow. *When it arrives, can that be your contribution to the show? Cut the poles, try to raise it at home and then at school?*

Very good, he nodded.

It could be a great bonding activity with Stephen, I suggested. *Father and son.*

We'll see about that, he said as the bell rang.

A few weeks later, Dana texted two pictures. The first featured him, thankfully laughing, wearing a knit cap while scanning a pile of poles. I appreciated his humor as he tried to erect the tipi in his field, and I realized instantly someone else held the camera. The second photo presented a more organized Stephen ready to erect the tipi.

They worked together on it, I thought while viewing the pictures. I don't have any insight into Dana's parenting, but the task of sustainably felling saplings to build a tipi for school probably doesn't meet with much enthusiasm from many seventeen-year-old boys. That they spent a Saturday working together made me glad. When I walked into the auditorium

Monday afternoon, the tipi stood proud on the stage wing opposite the skeleton of the emerging pirate ship. On the Monday after the show, the tipi vanished, and I found it packed away backstage. An audience member had loved it and repaid us the full price of the tipi, again helping to financially sustain the program.

On Wednesday, March 14, 2018, I worked the library reference desk nightshift at the nearby community college when I received a text message from Kris:

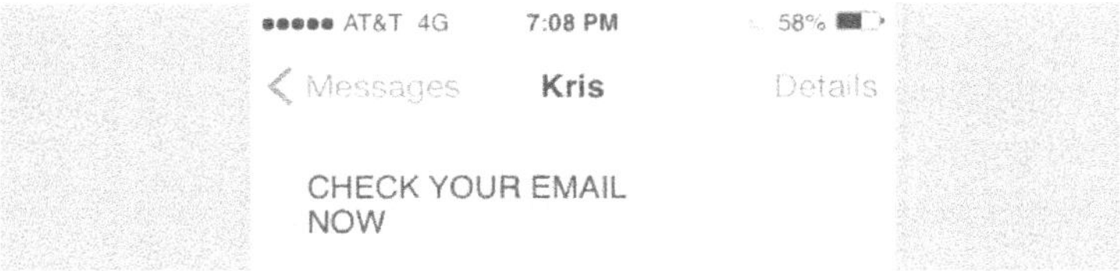

Fortunately, I didn't have a student patron in front of me, so I opened the app on my phone, the notifications for which I kept turned off. I saw an email from Kris in my inbox and the subject read: "Fwd: Oakmont Regional High School Musical." The urgency of his text, coupled with the ambiguity of the subject, made me nervous as I clicked and read: "Good afternoon Mason, Thank you for your phone call today. Here is the basic information regarding Peter Pan" and Kris outlined all the information I already knew about the union rate for orchestra musicians. So I replied to Kris:

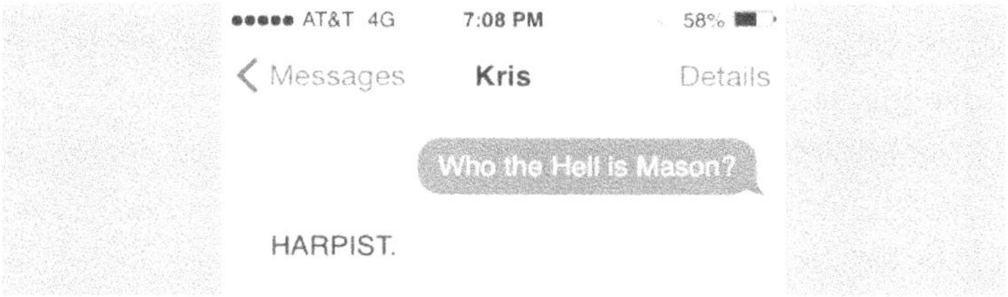

To this day, neither of us knows how Mason Morton got Kris's number. Kris had posted an advertisement for a harpist on musician's boards, Facebook, and made plenty of cold calls to orchestras, but we're not at all certain about the actual intervention with Mason—except for one piece. Sharon made quite a few calls herself and, with the late hour of the production, she said a prayer. While I'd like to think that God listens to prayers, I'm not at all sure; but if he does, I have no doubt God listens to the prayers of Sharon Sawtell.

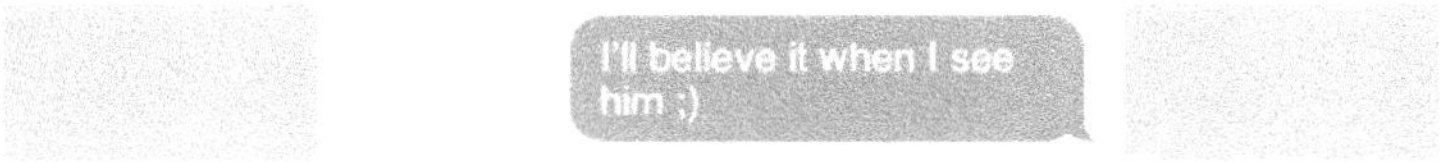

Kris didn't respond to my chide.

On Sundays during the musical season, I sent a weekly email to the adult creative team and another to the student cast (sometimes along with their parents) to remind them what was in store for the week ahead, any approaching deadlines, and to inspire some motivation for our work. Normally I composed these emails in the evening, but on the morning of Sunday, March 18—just four days after the good news from Mason—I wrote from my dining room table. My phone rang seconds after sending the staff email. The screen showed Kris's photo and number. He and I talk throughout the school day either in person or by text, but rarely on the phone, so, I answered. He broke the news after I said hello.

My dad died.

Oh Kris, I'm so sorry. I, er. I had no idea—you were just...you said he was ok, did I miss something?

He explained that the news shocked him, too. Kris isn't one for sharing too many personal details, but I struggled to place the events in order. I could not comprehend the situation, nor could he, it turned out. He said that his dad had been weaker in February than on the cruise the previous summer, but there had been no immediate sign of decline then. In the intervening month or so, his dad grew weaker and slipped away that night.

Jenn and I are going to Florida to help, I'm not sure for how long.

Of course. I'm shocked Kris. Just tell me what you need, ok?

Thanks, Jeff.

Kris rarely misses school, so his two-week absence proved a major hurdle for him and the entire school. His family held a memorial service in Florida where his parents had moved twenty years earlier, and then everyone returned to Massachusetts for another memorial. Kris has three brothers and a very active mother—nothing appeared small about the funeral that unfolded. Kris' absence became an unfillable hole for us: the music ensembles and classes lacked their maestro, the 400 wing fell quiet without our jester, meetings of the faculty—either at the lunch table or in the conference room—convened with one of the great leaders of the school absent, and on stage, we all truly missed our music director with just over a month to go before curtain. Time, just as for Captain Hook, weighed heavily on my mind that March both practically and existentially.

Despite the difficulty of the situation, everyone helped make those weeks easier. Sharon rehearsed with us and reviewed our past work but we avoided learning new music without Kris, so we focused on new choreography with Karen. The kids, however, proved to be the most heroic. As many of them also performed in Kris's ensembles, they understood the difficulty of what little we tried to accomplish without him, and they responded to the constant adjustments and my own limitations in those weeks. I remember thanking them in one of my post-rehearsal pep talks—*You can tell we're a family when someone is missing, can't you?* I said, and watched sixty-or-so teenage heads gently nod in response—many, like me, with tears in their eyes.

When deaths happen among the Oakmont faculty, or retirees, or even family, there's a healthy discussion about who from school should attend the funeral because, while so many of us would want to attend, someone needs to steer the ship at school. I told Mr. Uminski that I would like to go to Mr. DeMoura's Massachusetts memorial, and he agreed. Sharon also attended with me and we had a mid-day window of time to drive to Reading—about an hour from school—for the funeral and back before rehearsal. Sharon was so thoughtful she even made me a brown-bag lunch to eat before rehearsal began.

I found it a great comfort to sit with Sharon in the pew of the Baptist Church and to share this moment with the DeMoura family. Sharon looked peaceful, undoubtedly in prayer, while I scanned the congregation for Oakmont alumni who attended to support Kris. Both my head and heart pounded. As the family entered the church, I leaned over to Sharon and asked, *What size t-shirt do you think Kris' kids are? I need to order them and I don't want to ask.* She smiled, gave me her best motherly guess, and I pushed the lengthy to-do list from my mind to share the somber moment with the family and congregation.

"To die will be an awfully big adventure," says Peter Pan in Act III of the original play. In the midst of mourning someone so clearly loved as Mr. Samuel DeMoura, it's hard to see anything bright in the darkness of death. Yet eulogist after eulogist spoke so eloquently to Mr. DeMoura's kindness, gentleness, and respectability. In reading Peter Pan's words literally, death is that great unknown journey we all must take, and so it truly becomes an adventure for us all. Given his fervent faith, I suspect he anticipated his onward journey. At least I'd like to think as much. The events of late March had surely interrupted the production, but in a way that reminded me that all of us involved—students, teachers, parents, and staff—share in that other-worldly adventure and that the legacy of our unique work becomes a part of the greater whole of our being, and a part of our families—including the families that are the cast, school, and community.

I infrequently make decisions in the program without consulting Kris, but I made one in the weeks after his father's passing. His mother remained in Massachusetts for a month and traveled among her sons' homes. She and her son Kenny joined us at the Friday night performance of *Peter Pan.* As I introduced the show from the deck of the pirate ship, I made sure not to look Kris in the eyes. *A few weeks ago,* I explained to the audience, *we lost a member of our community—someone I never had the privilege to meet. How lucky we are, however, to have his son and his son's family in our schools every day. So tonight, on behalf of our students and my colleagues, and all of us here with his wife Jean, we dedicate this performance of Peter Pan to the memory of Mr. Samuel DeMoura.* Rarely have I heard applause as beautiful—either in Alumni Auditorium or elsewhere—and the moment confirmed for me yet another reason why this program, in this school, is different from the others I've known elsewhere. I don't write better, just different.

My sister texted after the funeral to try and lift my spirits.

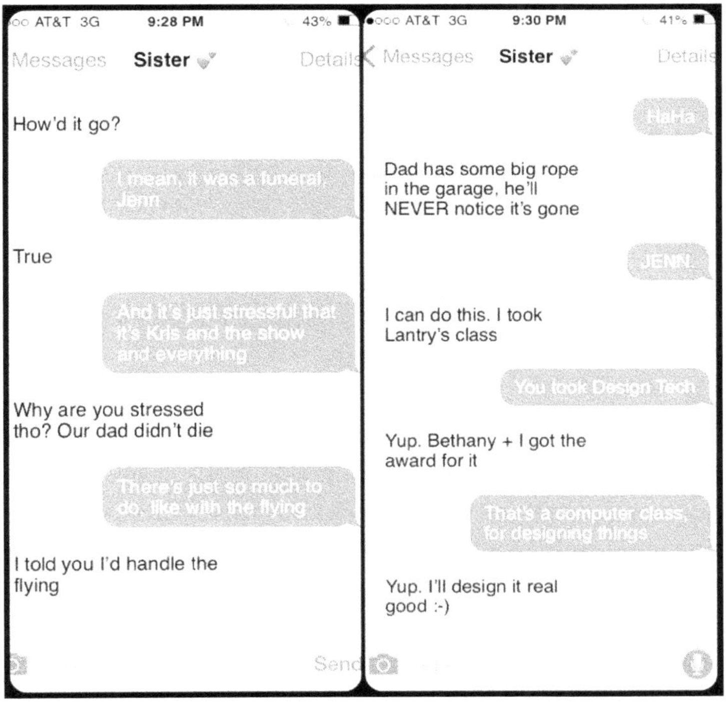

Creating Neverland took more than a pirate ship and a tipi. While the backdrops provided color and a sense of space for the London skyline and the Neverland forest, I still needed to create a nursery for the Darling home and the underground house for the Lost Boys (and Girls). Before I applied for the AWFAE grant, Kris connected me with a local artist, Tom Simahk, whose sons Tyler and Sam actively participated in Oakmont Theatre. Tom's wife Bonnie, an Oakmont alumna, also helped provide community input for the Mass Humanities grant. Tom is a gentleman, father, and eager to solve problems creatively. His craftsmanship for the stage rivals Dave's. With help from AWFAE, Tom worked with me and some students to create a nursery window through which Peter would fly, as well as a spectacular underground house plucked right from the pages of a storybook, complete with trapdoors and secret entrances. Tom's artistry lends well to the stage—he uses large strokes and bold colors to capture the essential without worrying about details hidden from the audience. Like Dave, Tom and I started with a big idea and he delivered spectacularly, while the kids helped and painted and had fun shaping their own set. Tom played another indispensable role on the team, which we could not have afforded without AWFAE.

I really wanted to sleep in on Saturday, March 24, even with the sunny skies and the spring air waking the sleeping flora. Passover and Easter fell just a week away, which always signals the start of spring for me regardless of their date of celebration. Online ticket pre-sales began that morning for the families of cast members. Anxiety had continued to mount over ticket availability, so when I arrived at my local Starbucks for my first morning coffee, I logged on to the website and saw that some eager parents had already bought sizable blocks of tickets. Even better, I didn't have any emails about ticket problems and things worked fine as I drove west on Massachusetts Route 2 for my meeting with Jasmine Goodfellow in Amherst.

Not only does this quaint New England town connect five area colleges—Amherst, Hampshire, Mount Holyoke, Smith, and UMass—it's also known for its controversial name. When the town became incorporated in 1759, Massachusetts Governor Thomas Pownall named the settlement for his friend, Lord Jeffrey Amherst, British commander in North America during the Seven Years' War (1756-1763). Students generally remember Lord Amherst for distributing of smallpox-infested blankets to groups of indigenous peoples during Pontiac's Rebellion in 1763. Given this dishonorable legacy, some (as recently as 2018) have called for the town to be renamed. In 2016, Amherst College—where Lisa Brooks, whom I emailed about the Humanities project, teaches—replaced "Lord Jeff" with a mammoth as their school mascot, while at town meeting, residents voted to rename the federal holiday known as Columbus Day as Indigenous Peoples' Day in town. Residents of Amherst, in a way similar to us at Oakmont, tried to both cling to some traditions while also acknowledge the past pain inflicted on indigenous groups—in this case, by Lord Amherst. The controversy gnawed at me as I drove to meet Jasmine, the UMass theatre student whom Larry Spotted Crow Mann recommended. We met at the Pleasant Street Starbucks, just north of the Amherst common, to discuss the project.

Jasmine presented herself far more mature than most college students; she spoke purposefully and thoughtfully with her soft voice. After getting her a latte, we talked a bit about her theatre work and a new musical she had produced entitled *1675* about the tragedy of Deer Island when, during King Philip's War, colonists forcibly moved some 500 Nipmucs from eastern Massachusetts to an empty strip of land in Boston Harbor. Jasmine clearly brought historical, as well as dramatic, insight to her work and ours. She had heard, from her uncle Larry Spotted Crow Mann as well as read on Facebook, the frustration that some members of her Nipmuc nation had with our project. *But it's a sweet play,* she reassured me. Jasmine encouraged our project from the start and drew on her experience at UMass where the theatre program similarly tried to grapple with the problem of racial stereotyping in theatre. *Try a headdress of flowers for Tiger Lily instead of feathers*, she pointed out, *with lots of flowers and earth tones in the costumes rather than buckskin, like this,* she said as she sketched in my little *Peter Pan* notebook.

What about the Ugg-a-Wugg song? I asked.

It's got to go. With the juvenile pidgin English.

But the contract?

Keep the song, it's all about friendship, just drop the stupid words. There have been worse adaptations.

What about a show-stopper? I pressed.

I don't like the idea. It won't work for the performers or the audience.

This had been Karen's point. I wanted to align with Bob Goodby who saw this as the time to make a bold statement, but as Karen had argued and Jasmine now agreed, the kids' performance must take center stage. The show needed a teaching moment for sure, but it remained a scripted—and contracted—performance nonetheless.

A short statement at the end, giving another side to the story. Not a long oration, just a voice, Jasmine suggested.

Would you be willing to be that voice? I asked, hopefully.

Gladly. She smiled, like a good friend.

Nine months had passed since I first reached out to Bob Goodby and only one month remained to pull all the pieces of the complex project together. Many times I thought I had lost the thrust of the Humanities work and it had served as nothing but a distraction. We might have just copied the nearby school with their production and never considered the problem at all. A year later, I asked Kris what he thought about the Humanities work and he responded without hesitation:

We did the right thing; absolutely. We're in the business of educating, we weren't going to stop educating because of resistance.

He reminded me that it wasn't the first time Oakmont had to deal with the problem.

Remember when it came up in Millie? he asked, referring to the 2014 production of *Thoroughly Modern Millie*. *There was a satirical scene with the Chinese immigrants. The show did ok on Broadway, but it didn't sit right with our administration. They brought in an outsider to talk to the kids and wrote a bit in the playbill about understanding different people of different time periods. The Mass Humanities work was so much better, the kids understood from the start why it was a problem, how we were sensitive to it, and how the community felt about it. It was great.*

Jasmine shared many ideas about costumes and props and we agreed to plan the details for her short closing statement in the coming weeks. I left Amherst with so much gratitude: for Larry's introduction to Jasmine, for the scope of the Humanities work, and for the many kind people who wanted help the kids learn and grow. I called Karen as soon as I sat in the car.

Great news! It couldn't have gone better.

Wonderful! How can I help? she asked. Karen, as always, radiated positivity.

First, choreograph the Ugg-a-Wugg song however you'd like, just know it will be all instrumental without the meaningless words.

Oh, that's such a relief, Jeff. Thank you, thank you.

Let's incorporate lots of handshakes and flowers, though, to represent friendship. Jasmine liked flowers.

I love it.

I need costume help. Doreen has all the comic book buckskin things but that won't work for us.

What do you need?

Floral. Whimsical. Bright ballet, but cheap. Am I making sense?

I've got it. Give me an hour. Make it an hour-and-a-half, I've got to walk the dogs.

You can have the weekend, Karen. But thank you, as always.

What did she say about the show-stopper?

It's out. We agree with you, Karen, it would distract the kids.

Oh, I'm so relieved, thank you.

No, thank you, Karen.

My pleasure.

Karen stayed true to her word. By the time I arrived home she had texted pictures of an elegant, whimsical leotard with a skirt. I responded while sitting in my Jeep in the garage.

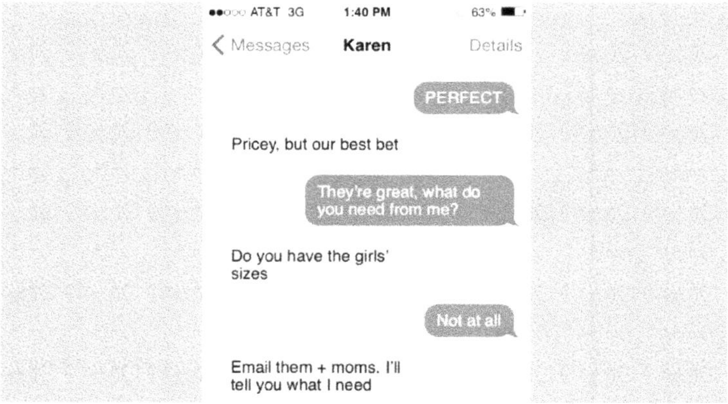

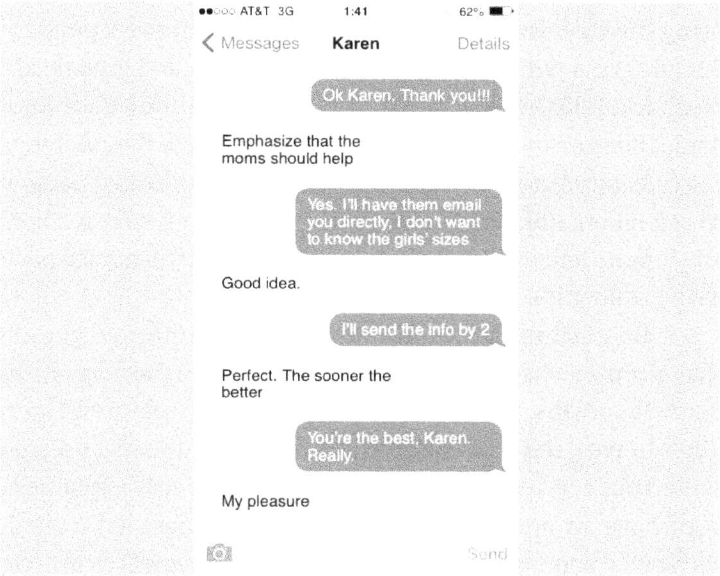

Karen surpassed the terms of her job description with those costumes. She handled everything and the dresses fit perfectly. The girls matched identically in their whimsical, earth-tone patterns, except for Tiger Lily who, in her crown of daisies, wore scarlet to befit a princess. The scenes worked better than I could have dreamed, and Karen—not me—brought Jasmine's good vision to life. We continued to make progress as Kris returned from his leave that week and we all hurriedly moved towards the end of March.

After meeting with Jasmine, I felt I had a grip—maybe for the firs time—on the Humanities project. Kris dug into the score to make sure the orchestra could carry us without vocals and Karen choreographed the number. As the grant funds covered educational components—not production costs—I had to bring the steering committee back to Oakmont to respond to our progress with the "Ugg-a-Wugg" scene and give us all feedback. Bob Goodby, James Stanley, and Tammy Bucchino made themselves available for April 10 and, while they weren't the full committee, the date was the best for the most people to attend an afternoon rehearsal. In just two weeks we had all—adults and especially kids—pulled the performance part of the Humanities project together.

We did not run the whole show for the committee guests that afternoon because they only needed to see the parts with Barrie's Indians. Two dance numbers in Act II featured Tiger Lily's braves, the first featured just dance and the second presented our re-working of "Ugg-a-Wugg." As Kris explained, both have an underlying rhythmic figure, most associated with tribal sounds—a part sometimes stereotypical to Native American music. We ran both scenes with the surrounding dialogue. While we only had two weeks to work the latter number, I felt confident to present it to our guests. Still, I wanted to reassure the kids. I told them before we began that we would host some guests at the end of rehearsal, eliciting giggles. Apart from Tiger Lily, Peter, Wendy, and Liza none of the students had met the members of this group, despite having heard much about them. *They're not the theatre police*, I told the cast at the start of rehearsal. *They're teachers like Mr. DeMoura, or Sharon, or Karen—and they're here to help us grow. Many of you know Tammy from town, too.* A sea of teenage heads again nodded in their seats.

Our guests arrived on time and we ran the numbers with Sharon at the piano. I loved Karen's use of handshakes and the exchange of flowers in the dance. Each Lost Boy or Girl handed a silk daisy to a brave—and then back—symbolizing their friendship. In writing this story, I've asked colleagues, students, friends, community members about all sorts of aspects of the show; but I saved a very special question for some of the students with whom I've worked the longest and closest. I asked them about my friendship with Kris, which was so representative of the friendship I wanted to portray among the kids on stage. There's a joke that we're like Rodgers and Hammerstein, the former the composer and the latter the dramatist. The words of one student struck me more than any other research I did for the book. Madyson, a student I twice taught in class and who actively participates in both theatre and in the music program, wrote: "we see the relationship you two have and it inspires us to be as kind and friendly to each other. Your friendship rubs off on us in ways that make us feel safe and wanted." She played a Lost Girl searching for belonging in *Peter Pan* and danced enthusiastically with Tiger Lily's braves. The following year, in *Evita*, she played a nun to her parents' great delight—just as her older sister Brooke had played in *The Sound of Music.*

The kids sat in the auditorium seats while the guests addressed them after the performance. *I've never seen* Peter Pan, Bob Goodby confessed from the start. *I've read about it for this project, and I'm excited to see your production in a few weeks. You've done really well.* He then explained the significance of the issue and the importance of the Humanities work. *The parts I saw don't poke fun at native peoples, but there was one line that made me a little uncomfortable. Does anyone know?*

I sure as hell didn't. I started to panic. Then a courageous hand went up in the darkness—I don't even remember whose.

The line about the peace pipe.

Exactly, said Bob. He explained the significance of the peace pipe in indigenous culture and how, in the story, the reference was too lighthearted—especially Peter's accompanying dialogue in pidgin English. *If I may, Mr. Aubuchon, how about saying "we make peace" instead of "we smoke peace pipe?"*

Brilliant, I said from the back of the auditorium, while slightly fearing a breach of contract with the licensor.

Tammy spoke next, always genuine and kind. Many of the students knew her as a mom and neighbor. She shared her story about going to Oakmont just like them but also growing-up different because of her native heritage—something that she proudly shares with others like she did that day. She, too, praised the kids for making their work authentic and treating the topic seriously and agreed with Bob's observation about the peace pipe. Her words offered nothing but gratitude to the kids of her community for their effort. I beamed with pride, not only for the kids' efforts, but to have worked with my classmate—Tammy—on this project.

James Stanley walked on stage in a way that wholly befit a professor of theatre. He spoke briefly about authenticity in a performer's work, but everyone remembered him for standing upstage—in a dark and bare space—and slowly walking toward the audience literally filling the stage with his presence. No microphone, no makeup, just a tall, thin teacher showing sixty or so students how an actor's presence can fill an entire auditorium. He also articulated his message to the kids: choose the authentic over the silly when storytelling.

For all my worry, the experience could not have gone better. The guests provided real feedback to the cast and they validated the kids' hard work. The months of research and agonizing about whether or not we walked the right path resolved itself that afternoon. The next morning, however, I found real peace with the work. I received an email from a senior member of the cast, Lauren, who joined the ensemble in her last year of high school simply to be a part of the production. I didn't know Lauren well but she wrote sincerely:

> Hi Mr. Aubuchon,
>
> As a right-minded person, PC [politically correct] policies have always resonated with me as a consequence of our sensitive, careful society. At the beginning of rehearsal back in January, I complained to my friends about what I thought was oversensitivity involving the Indians. I thought, it's an old play for kids, why is this so serious? However, after yesterday my perspective has changed completely. Hearing the speakers' opinions, I felt insensitive ... for my previous thoughts. I feel enlightened about the topic, and I understand your reasoning. I am so thankful for ... the chance to be a part of something so kind. Every artistic and technical decision ... has been extremely deliberate and considerate to both the Native American community and the audience. I just wanted to thank you for ... giving us the opportunity to express these ideas of friendship and imagination in an entertaining, beautiful way. How to make an ugly play beautiful? Add some flowers! Thank you for helping us all fly!

I shared Lauren's words with my thank you note to Bob, James, and Tammy. The project successfully resonated with the students like Lauren. As Kris always stressed, we had made the story ours and including voices beyond our own; I was proud. Tammy wrote in response: "I know we discussed teaching Native American heritage to the students back at the initial meeting. I feel they have learned something far greater than some old traditions. It makes my heart happy that the opportunity to teach has been grasped fully. I look forward to the show.... Break a leg, Tammy."

Both resistance and resolution became the momentum that sustained our production of *Peter Pan*. The constant back and forth, like the rocking of the moored *Jolly Roger* in the Neverland lagoon, exhausted me; however, notes like Tammy's gave me hope that this effort, and the effort that so many adults like Tammy and Jim or Dave and Karen, steered us straight through the scariest storms.

Act II, Scene 5: Dave

Precious few tickets remained when online sales began on April 1 between the seats earmarked for the children's performance, HOPE House, the Beacon of Hope, and Friends Club guests. I secured tickets for faculty, alumni, and the Lantry family for the Saturday night dedication. I also scrounged to find seats for the engineering students who had built the ship with Dave since some of these students had never attended a musical before. On Monday, the marquis at the end of the Oakmont driveway read: "PETER PAN TICKETS ON SALE NOW AWRSD WEBSITE." Special Education teacher James Mellekas and his students in the EXCEL Program, many of whom belong to the Friends Club, change the sign letters both as a learning experience and as a service to the school. By Friday they had to again change the sign to read: "PETER PAN TICKETS SOLD OUT." Some angry emails from ticketless people accompanied the good news of our sold-out show. I served as a clearinghouse for people who wanted to exchange tickets with others, but I neither anticipated nor, in the end, wanted the headache. I tried to remember that people wanted to share our journey to Neverland and I tried my best to accommodate everyone.

Friday afternoon rehearsals were generally tough, although

that time minimized conflict with other extracurricular activities. After a full week of teaching or learning, a two-and-a-half-hour rehearsal wore on us all. I sat in seat J9 that day, April 6, as Kris and Karen ran a dance number. My clipboard and dog-eared score rested on my knee with its yellow sticky notes. Everything looked good on stage, but I struggled to keep my eyes open. My phone buzzed and displayed a message from Mimi, who rejects capitalization as much as capitalism when texting (from her iPhone):

Her mother had, in fact, bought a ticket for her, just in case she decided to return home. My spirit lifted. For a little show in rural Massachusetts, people planned to travel far: Mimi would journey from Paris, John from L.A., my family from Vermont, and some of my closest friends—Danielle, Rob, and Parker—would drive from Virginia. I learned that family members of students would travel from as far away as New Jersey, Florida, and Ohio. Kris always responded the same way when I mentioned travelers: *Don't disappoint them.*

Thursday, April 12 was a quiet evening and I remember the lengthening sunrays stretching well into the dinner hour when I received an unexpected text message and picture from

Admiral Lantry: *Your ship, Sir.*

Captain Hook's Jolly Roger

I was awestruck. Dave delivered the ship a day ahead of schedule and at budget—thanks to the generosity of the faculty and the Blessington Corporation. While the kids had made great progress, I hadn't focused on the delivery date; I simply had too many things to juggle in my mind knowing they made reasonable progress. I went right to the auditorium when I arrived at school at 6:30 the next morning. Although I had watched the kids' work all season, I failed to comprehend what I saw standing there at that moment as the auditorium lights flickered on. The completed ship, built by a master teacher and his growing students, smashed right through the auditorium wall. The sails—sewn not by Mr. Smee but by Mrs.

Lantry—hung perfectly, needing only a breeze to move them; a figurehead skeleton reached across the prow while a retractable plank emerged from a concealed door, and portholes gave it all authenticity.

A skeleton figurehead, without clamshells, and a hidden plank extended high above the audience.

A boater himself, Dave carved a registration plate for the bow: BAS2018.

BAS2018? I asked walking into the shop to shake his hand.

Yeah. B-A-S. Big Ass Ship.

Ha. That's perfect. You know what it needs, though?

What?

A cannon. That fires t-shirts. Dave had built a PVC cannon that fired t-shirts into the gym audience at events using compressed air, and I envisioned similar. *The cannon was called "Long Tom" in the book.*

I bet it was. Long Tom will be installed by the end of the day. He beamed like a child on a Welsh Christmas.

Aye, aye, Admiral. I saluted.

Unprompted, I asked people to use one word to describe their immediate reaction when they discovered the *Jolly Roger*. "Holy shit, is that real?" asked Kris's seventy-eight-year-old mother, Jean—refusing, like her son, to limit herself to a single word. His father-in-law, Reggie, simply said "wow," while Reggie's wife, Cindi, called it "amazing" along with her daughter—Kris's wife Jenn. They all enjoyed good company in their disbelief as another mom, Carrie Tobia, called it "astounding." Tim Caouette called it "impressive," although Tim qualified his adjective as "massively impressive." Tim's wife, Jessica, saw it as "genius." When I asked my sister Jenn what word popped into her mind on seeing it, she didn't hesitate to say: "Lantry."

Other observers chose words that spoke to the fantastic nature of the project. Oakmont Vice Principal Kristina Bogosh thought it defied belief, calling it "incredible." A student, Jack, put the work on an Homeric scale and referred to the ship as "epic." Moms also utilized the vocabulary of fantasy: my mother said it was fabulous (as in fable-like), Sue O'Connor, considered it "spectacular," while Kelly Behringer liked "marvelous." I agree with these preternatural descriptions.

More than a year later, when I remember standing on the ship decks, or when I show pictures of it to new friends, the *Jolly Roger* speaks to me of the legendary; because, while neither the myth of pure fiction nor the fact of recorded history, legends bridge one to the other. Soon, the *Jolly Roger* will be the stuff of legends, and both those who swung hammers, as well as those who sang notes on those decks, will have graduated; the story of what they built will fade—as Grizabella sings in CATS—into memory.

We had not rehearsed on the ship during construction, so a major part of that afternoon's work became re-blocking ship scenes. Exhaustively, I ensured that every pirate got the chance to act on the ship at least once in the show and, while Dave designed the interior skeleton of steel, he cautioned me about having too many kids stand on the decks at once. We agreed to eight students or, as he said, *ten freshmen evenly distributed.*

As we wrapped the last pre-vacation rehearsal, I helped some students in the final moments before departing and stepped out of the auditorium. Sharon motioned to me when I returned to the nearly-empty auditorium moments later and I walked toward the piano.

I don't know her name, she whispered, *but a girl asked me to take her picture on the ship.*

Oh? I asked.

I hope that's ok. She was very careful up there.

Of course, I smiled, *but why did she want a picture?*

She said she wanted to remember the first time she got to stand on the ship.

I nearly wept. So much work had gone into that project from fundraising, to design, to construction, and then incorporating it into the story. Many people helped, foremost Dave and June, make that dream a reality and so many people since that day, when commenting on the production have said "and that ship!" I asked another student, Olivia, whom I knew from class, about the ship. Although she's an active dancer and student of Karen's, Liv has never been able to fit the musical into her spring schedule—most understandably as one of Oakmont's strongest student leaders. I wanted her opinion on the ship, as a non-member of Oakmont Theatre who remains passionate about all things Oakmont (like her brothers and her dad, Chris). "Together," she wrote. "Our ship was built together. The show was built together. It was a community project that couldn't have happened and had the effect it did without everyone working TOGETHER, no matter how big or how small of a role they put in." Liv could not have been more right about that and, indeed, the ship symbolized the production as a whole and the many people who brought it into being. We didn't just fly to Neverland, we sailed there on our ship made of dreams.

Creating and editing the playbill also consumed much of my time during the musical season. Thankfully, Mrs. Ina Carey gave me tremendous help with the work, even after her children graduated. Her daughter, Shale, played a nun as a senior in *The Sound of Music* and her son Max played Eugene in *Grease* and then Mr. Darling in *Peter Pan.* Additionally, both she and her husband Tom came out of their empty nest to coach the new generation of parent volunteers in concession sales at *Evita.* The Carey family of Westminster remains, without question, indispensable to Oakmont Theatre, and everything Ina and Tom touch—including the playbill—turns golden. The advertising space in the book represents about one-third of production revenue, the other parts being ticket sales as well as grants and other fundraisers. Ina ensured playbill perfection, especially since advertisers paid up to $100 per ad.

As I explained at the pre-season parent meeting, every student had an equal quota of ad revenue to generate, simply calculated by subtracting the program's fund balance plus reasonable revenue expectations from the overall budget and dividing the shortfall by the anticipated number of cast members. The flying costs in *Peter Pan* added significant expense and each student had to raise $200 in 2018; but because of the success of *Peter Pan* and exceeded revenue expectations, and because *Evita* was a smaller show to produce (Eva didn't fly, after all), each student only had to raise $125 in 2019. Compare that to the District-imposed activity fee that required athletes and members of extracurricular music ensembles to pay close to $400 per season. In Oakmont Theatre, because the program was self-funding, about half of the families would pay the amount by writing a check and not sell advertisements, which was also perfectly acceptable. The fee also included two tickets per performance for the students' loved ones to attend. The other half of families would call on local businesses and parents' business contacts. School administrators, teachers in various departments, and even the teachers' association all regularly purchased advertisements to help the program, usually with a message of encouragement to the cast. Some parents also bought ad space and incorporated baby photos or candid pictures in their message of support for their student.

I scrutinized cast lists, staff lists, lists of musical numbers, words of thanks, a dedication and an *In Memoriam* page, as well as the language required by the contract before Ina proofread the book. I then reread it to get it perfect. This was no brochure—the *Peter Pan* playbill ran a full seventy-two pages with no blank space.[11] Engineering teacher Greg Secino and business teacher Wendy LeBlanc helped print mock copies before hand-delivering the file to the Graphic Communications department at the nearby Montachusett Regional Vocational Technical High School, whose students generously printed the bills at cost under the direction of Mr. Brian Bean, making the document a true community product.

Statements from each of the scholars explaining the Humanities project became significant components of the *Peter Pan* playbill. I wanted the audience to read from the perspective of Dr. Goodby and Dr. Stanely—experts in their respective fields of archaeology and theatre—how we at Oakmont approached the challenge of indigenous representation. Both scholars explained in their writing how student remained at the heart of this project. Not locked in the ivory tower of academia, both Bob and James drew on the experience of their visits to Oakmont and their active engagement with our students, proving themselves master teachers.

Dr. Goodby put the concern for the project squarely with the people of Ashburnham and Westminster. "For Native Americans in our community and student body controversies ranging from the use of Indian mascots by sports teams to whether we should celebrate Christopher Columbus are particularly painful," he wrote. "In addition to presenting a familiar and cherished story, our version of Peter Pan also addresses difficult issues of cultural diversity, ethnic stereotyping, and racism by questioning the play's derogatory portrayal of Native Americans." He continued by explaining our solution and giving the audience an invitation: "We have intentionally chosen not to remove the offensive content and create a safe, sanitized version of the play; instead, we ask you, our audience, to reflect on questions of identity, history, and social justice in ways that promote respectful discussion." I particularly appreciated his use of "our" and "we" in the statement; this had been a journey on which Bob had joined us and our dialogue with the members of the Native American community had greatly benefited from hearing his voice at the table. The concise statement illuminated the road we had traveled together.

The kids had loved Dr. Stanley's stage demonstration. To be fair, James not only taught theatre at Harvard, but he also enjoys a successful acting career as well. The father of young children himself, he kept a magnetic rapport with the kids while presenting the complexity of the representation problem: "Acting asks performers to inhabit worldviews other than their own, to empathize with the experiences of those unlike themselves. When actors approach a text uncritically, they risk perpetuating the biases of that text, just as adventure literature perpetuated the biases of that age through caricature," he wrote, explaining that we at Oakmont chose another road. We had "chosen to engage with this text not only as a play to be enjoyed but also as an historical artifact to be analyzed and interrogated.... At a moment in which these actors are themselves exploring new ways of being in the world, they generously offer us a chance to join them, in the hopes that we can all learn and grow up a bit, together." I appreciate that he never called them students but always addressed them as actors in their own right. Both James and Bob confirmed for Kris and I that, as educators, we had walked the right path of learning and growing. Indeed, a neighboring school produced *Peter Pan* the same year as we, with none of the same work in cultural awareness. I suspect we might have similarly slipped by without making the same headlines as in *The New York Times*. For me, however—and I suspect Kris, too—this wouldn't have been right. Learning from Dr. Goodby and Dr. Stanley remained essential to our journey and raised important awareness not only for us and the actors involved but also the history students who participated in the post-matinee discussion. We all found ourselves growing up.

My inbox filled rapidly during musical season, increasingly as opening night approached. I was challenged to sort through the diversity of requests: will these shoes work for Betty? Did you update the mailing address for the trombonist? Are there two center seats available for Friday night? Answering these requests is, of course, part of the job and in addition to the typical emails about homework and faculty meetings I get in the normal course of a day. On Wednesday, April 18—ten days before opening night and just three before vacation—I received an unsolicited email that added unanticipated stress.

The very polite and brief email came from a woman named Daniella Zalcman, who introduced herself as a "documentary photographer working on a project for *National Geographic Magazine* on Native American representation." She had heard of our story and she wanted to photograph the production for her December article. Typically, I forwarded the email to Kris and set off down the hall to his office, I raced so quickly I think I arrived before the message.

What's this? I'm just seeing it now, he said sitting at his desk.

For the Humanities project. National Geographic. This woman read about the work somewhere.

Congrats.

Not congrats. This is getting too big, Kris.

Seems it. Did you talk to Mr. Uminski?

No, it just arrived. I need a plan before I talk to him.

What are you going to do? She seems nice enough.

Remember how this all started? The headline: School Pulls Plug on Peter Pan?

I know.

What should I do?

He paused and looked at his desk with its awards and pictures of his family. *The same thing we've been doing from the start: providing the best educational experience for our kids.*

He was right.

It's not just about the show, or the Humanities project, I said.

Of course not.

It's about teaching the kids about community. Sharing our story.

I agree.

I don't want an outsider getting in the way.

Hang on, you've sold 1600 tickets to "outsiders," Jeff. The show is for the public.

I know. Let's tell the story about selling all the seats.

Frame it as a lesson: what's the objective?

Students will be able to....

In your own words, jerk.

To demonstrate an understanding of the problem of misrepresentation on stage.

Correct.

I got burned in the fall. I don't want protestors in the driveway.

Neither do I. Don't forget, I live in this town—you don't.

Kris was right about that, too—the stakes were higher for him and his family.

She doesn't sound like a protestor. She's a journalist.

I agree. I stood there, unable to find a way forward. *There's just so much to do, in just ten days.*

We can't go back now, Jeff. I don't want to go back. Let her tell—no, help her tell—this story.

We've had serious pushback. I've got some seriously angry email.

Hell ya. But you've also made friends. Allies. Goodby and Stanley—you respect them, right?

Yes.

They're completely on board. As is Dana. As is Mr. Uminski. Both are educators you respect believe in this project. And the meeting, although rough, came to a good resolution.

True.

What about Tammy?

What about Tammy? I asked.

She's a mom. She's a grad. She was your classmate here. She's proud of her native heritage and she's an active member of the community. She's been behind this project since day one. Trust her instinct, it's good.

You're right, I said.

What are you going to do?

Tell Mr. Uminski National Geographic is coming to his school.

He'll tell you that's perfect.

No shit, Kris. Everything is perfect to him until it isn't.

I found Mr. Uminski in the cafeteria. Like me, he also eats school lunch most days. More than eating tater tots, however, one of his great strengths as principal is his visibility to students during lunches and in the hallways, where kids have no qualms about approaching him. I told him about Daniella as he stood, eating, and supervising 350 students alongside two green-bleeding Oakmonters: Mr. Fitzgerald and Mr. Dawley of the Athletic department who both support school artists as much as their athletes.

What does she need from us? Mr. Uminski asked.

She didn't say, but I'll ask.

Sounds good. Are you going to say yes?

I'm going to talk to the grant committee just to make sure they are ok with it.

Perfect. He gave me a thumbs up. *Oh, I saw your paperwork for the CATS field-trip in January.*

Oh, yes, is there a problem? I asked.

No, not at all, but don't you hate CATS?

That's DeMoura.

Oh. Perfect. Mr. Uminski nodded and returned to his tray.

After school, I sent an email to the committee and overnight both Bob Goodby and Tammy Bucchino responded. They shared my concerns but also agreed that we should tell our story. None of us found any indication that Daniella practiced "gotcha journalism"—nor did she—so we welcomed her like any guest. The people whom I respected agreed that this presented a good opportunity, so I responded to Daniella and invited her to photograph the dress rehearsal as well as attend Saturday's post-matinee forum. Daniella explained that she needed media releases for any students photographed. I didn't have time to track down sixty-two signatures with just, by that time, eight days until the dress rehearsal. I appealed to Mr. U. who characteristically said, *I'll take care of it.* And he did.

I told the kids at Friday's rehearsal we would welcome a visitor from *National Geographic Magazine.* Again their eyes widened as they whispered among themselves.

People are responding to what you're giving the world. Remem-

ber that, I said, *and let's keep it fantastic.*

While February vacation felt like an interruption, April vacation was a treasure and, in 2018, I needed it more than ever. I wanted to ignite some enthusiasm before the kids left for their own vacations and I initially thought to distribute 750 green Frisbees that read "never grow up" as the kids ran to the buses.

In my mind, I'm seeing South Ash Road littered with green plastic Frisbees as I drive away from school, Jeff, Vice Principal Kristina Bogosh said with a laugh when I floated the idea by her.

But it's all about flying Kris.

Oh, I get it, Jeff, she said, still laughing. I saw her point though.

While more expensive, green and black sunglasses with our Peter Pan logo looked pretty cool, especially for sunny April vacation. As the kids headed to the buses that Friday, cast members stood at the exits distributing the shades and telling their peers to *stay cool.* I also set some aside for the cast as well as students in the special education classrooms who often had different transportation arrangements. As promotional items, the glasses only needed to create short-term buzz, but the odd pair still appear every once in a while, and I smile when they do. The *Peter Pan* story celebrates frivolity and I tried to imbue the whole school with levity that spring while we grew.

I considered myself quite resourceful in managing the budget for *The Sound of Music* in 2016, in part because I didn't inherit detailed accounting records. With *Grease,* I budgeted for cast t-shirts and, as a way to show support, I quietly sold matching t-shirts at cost to faculty and staff. During the school day of opening night in 2017, not only did fifty-five students wear red and white Rydell High shirts, but thirty of their teachers did, too. That's more than ten percent of the school sporting varsity-style Rs around the school, which led to some good complaints from parents who also wanted t-shirts. For *Peter Pan* then, not only did the students and interested teachers have green t-shirts, but thanks to online sales, a good number of parents, grandparents, and even tiny students from the elementary schools bought them. The tiniest was a special order I had custommade for Miss Caia Caouette, age four. The online sales became a significant fundraiser for the program, selling 138 shirts in addition to those for the cast and staff. Again, on opening night, much of the school wore the shirts in solidarity with the student performers. The t-shirts were a relatively inexpensive visual sign of support for Oamont Theatre and another way we built community. I also learned that some of our most generous teachers bought extra shirts to give to eager students in school. The fun continued into the show when Dan and Nick—two of Admiral Lantry's engineering students—filled the t-shirt cannon with compressed air and launched two into the audience at each intermission, soaring from the ship's deck into the depths of the auditorium to be caught by eager fans.

These hundreds of "never grow up" green t-shirts were in addition, however, to a very limited edition set of black t-shirts that had the Captain's hook ripping through the back. I had these black shirts specially made for Admiral Lantry, Mermaid Lantry (his wife, June), Greg Secino and Demetrios Tyros his fellow engineering teachers, Dana, as well as the custodial crew. Like a concert t-shirt, I branded it the "Shore Tour" and gave them all fitting pirate names like Greybeard Secino and Maddog Max. As a reminder of the journey, I included the line: "it started with a fish." Not only did those teachers proudly wear their black crew t-shirts on opening night, Mike's custodial team—Steve, John, and Donna—did throughout the entire weekend as they contributed their own effort, by keeping the building spotlessly clean for our thousands of guests.

I cast Tinker Bell at the last minute, despite the importance of that role. Modern audiences expected a Disney-like Tinker Bell or even Julia Roberts from *Hook*, but Barrie described the fairy in 1904 simply as: "a ball of light, no bigger than Mrs. Darling's fist," and for our production, it required a still student seated in the orchestra with a green laser pointer. The perfect candidate presented herself to me after class one day when I announced I needed someone to take on the responsibility. Janelle was a bright history student, although shy by nature. Casting her as Tinker Bell enabled her to play a significant role in the production without having to step on stage, and she performed flawlessly.

Fairies, and Tinker Bell in particular, featured significantly not only in Barrie's story but also in the genre of the play. *Peter Pan* became part of a popular genre that began in 1823 with the English translation of Grimm's fairy tales and included Lewis Carroll's *Alice in Wonderland* in 1865 as well as a popular mid-century production of *A Midsummer Night's Dream* that harnessed increasingly—technical innovations of the Victorian theatre. In other words, *Peter Pan* wasn't a one-off, it formed part of a nineteenth-century fairy trend. The era only drew to a close after a century when Arthur Conan Doyle—of the methodical Sherlock Holmes fame—controversially defended some fabricated photographs purporting proof for the existence of fairies. *Peter Pan* fits into this turn-of-the-century fairy fascination that also served as an escape from anxiety-provoking realism on stage. Remember, Barrie presented

Mr. Darling as the calculating, nervous clerk working in a new, industrial-era office. Spectators thus applauded stage fairies to avoid modernity while at the same time celebrated the theatrical realism of Henrik Ibsen. The turn-of-the-century was a bifurcated world. Americans feared the reality of Kansas twisters and the evils of prairie populism while suspending belief to the land of Oz.

Barrie, however, did something novel and avant-garde with his fairy by breaking through the fourth wall of the stage. At the end of Act II in the musical, Peter turned to the audience and pleads with them to save the perishing Tinker Bell: "Her light is growing faint, and if it goes out, that means she is dead! Her voice is so low I can scarcely tell what she is saying. She says—she says she thinks she could get well again if children believed in fairies!" As Peter extended his arms to the audience in the darkness, Janelle perfectly set the green ball of light into Peter's hands, just as the latter famously asked the audience: "Do you believe in fairies? Say quick that you believe! If you believe, clap your hands!" The stage direction that follows is significant as Barrie acknowledged that "*Many clap, some don't, a few hiss.... But* TINK *is saved,*" and Peter concluded by returning the audience: "Oh, thank you, thank you, thank you! And now to rescue Wendy!" Quite significantly, this was the only moment when the audience is recognized in *Peter Pan*. The scene appears as inconsequential and yet, both for the story and for our production, bore great significance as our audiences fiercely applauded every time to prove their fervent belief. Sitting behind Dave and June at the Saturday night finale, I saw them, with their children and grandchildren, displaying their undying belief not only in fairies but especially in these students.

III

Part Three

In the third act, we return home to those who love us.

Act III, Scene 1: Jeff

Just before April vacation, with opening night around the corner, Mr. Uminski visited my classroom with some news. The student slated to perform as John Darling, he explained, would be unavailable for rehearsals during vacation—which included learning to fly. While the student could still participate in the show, these critical rehearsals became non-negotiable. I understood the situation; I could argue nothing. I immediately consulted with Kris; with only two weeks to go, we had to find a cast member capable of learning all of John's lines with the vocal range to match. In addition, the student needed to provide his own "flyer" as parents worked the ropes backstage and would rehearse over vacation. We had an idea but wanted to ensure the parent agreed before I asked the student. Kris called Shawn, who agreed to help fly his son. We quickly made the arrangements, averted crisis, and Simon stepped into the role of John with only a week to learn his lines.

I prefer scheduling the show in early April so that we can all rest over break, but some years that's quite impossible because of Easter and Passover—as with *Peter Pan*. While I needed April vacation to catch-up on grading essays, I also again needed to escape my New England life, but I found so much to do in such a short time. I used the vacation period advantageously and scheduled the flying equipment load-in from ZFX for the Friday of vacation week. The flyers, and their parents, would rehearse Saturday before a day-long full-cast run on Sunday. Production Week 2018 dovetailed with vacation. I knew that since I would find myself exhausted in late April, I should get away at the start of the week and return just in time to learn the mechanics of flying.

John's band *Faultlines* released a new album, *Bittersweet Revival*, parts of which John had played for me in London. I landed an invitation to the listening party in Los Angeles that first vacation weekend and I jumped at the chance to go. I saw quite a bit of John over those two days—we met for lunch Saturday on a rooftop restaurant in West Hollywood and again after his night gig. We also brunched the next morning at a place called Franklin & Co. before heading to the party.

How's the song coming? I asked over my Eggs Benedict.

Uh-huh, he said grinning, as he fiddled with his salad. He clearly wouldn't give away any secrets although, I came to find out later, the song remained unfinished at that point. We arranged that I would be as surprised as the kids at the debut: he would email the music to Kris, who would forward it to Sharon. John would practice with Sharon at school on Friday while I taught and keep the song a surprise. He quickly changed the discussion as we ate: *what are you doing tomorrow before your flight? Your last bit of freedom before the show?*

I'm headed to Palm Springs.

Fabulous. I love it there. What are you doing?

Looking at property.

His eyes bulged before he parroted my words: *Looking at property? In Palm Springs?*

Uh-huh.

Even before I signed the contract to produce *Evita* in 2019 or looked at the score, I knew the music well enough to know young Eva's line in the song *Buenos Aires*: "we'll put on a show." That tune often runs through my head during production week. When I returned from my trip, I had no time for post-California jet lag; we had to—in Eva's words—put on a show, and in a short time.

Russell Morgan arrived on Friday, April 20 from ZFX along with a crew of parents led by Keith Aubin to install the flying apparatus that waited for us in a large, wheeled freight container. Russell directed and Keith took mental notes for disassembling the rigging on the following Sunday. I busied myself tending to last-minute things before the kids and their parents arrived on Saturday for their first flight lesson. I had a few moments to read through my inbox, including confirming the bagpiper. Karen also came on Friday to help hang the backdrops and I also hung two 4' x 6' flags from the lobby rafters to greet the students on their return from April vacation: a Union Jack and a skull-and-crossbones—the week ahead would prove to be a grand adventure at Oakmont.

Students auditioning for flying roles had to provide one dedicated adult for all the shows to work their ropes. I didn't want anyone other than someone chosen by the students' family assuming the liability of helping their child fly. The experience became rather unique for a dad like Keith to hoist his son Kaden—who played Michael—high up into the air. I asked Keith about the experience, and he replied by email. "There was something unexplainable about it, honestly.... I think it was a carnival of the senses so to speak both visually and emotionally. And the fact that both our son and daughter were on stage, I may not have been the one flying BUT, I, too, flew in some strange way." Keith—himself ox-strong—also recalled what he termed the "bull work." He continued: "It's sobering, it's a proverbial trust fall every live pull, every show.... There was a bond created for all of us 'Men & Women in Black,'" he wrote, referring to the black crew t-shirts the parents wore. I was glad the parents agreed with my decision to use them as flyers.

The kids also worked themseles tired, starting early Saturday morning with Amanda and Mary. Karen, who doubles not only as choreographer and stage manager, but also stage mom, expertly fit the girls' harnesses. I did not anticipate how tired the kids grew while soaring through the air—after all, I've never flown myself. Kris said that the first time he saw Amanda fly put a smile on his face; conversely, I didn't relax until they all landed on their feet late on Saturday night.

Everything came together for the first time on Sunday, April 22. The flyers arrived early, around 10:00, for a couple of practices before the rest of the cast and the orchestra. We also added Doreen's costumes that Sunday and wanted to fit everything between noon and 5:00 pm. I'm grateful for the extra help I had during production week because it enabled me to delegate more tasks. Karen and Doreen expertly got everyone what they needed backstage while moving things along. I didn't have to worry about backstage because I had such capable women maintaining order. In the house, Kris talked with Sharon. Mike Rellstab, an Oakmont alumnus and our Technical Director, fitted the principals with their microphones. Kris scheduled the orchestra to arrive at 3:00, but I wanted to complete a run—with flying and Sharon on piano—before I had to pay the musicians. My phone read 12:10, but the day's chaos warranted the slight delay.

Everyone on stage please, I said, and Karen corralled them.

Kris led the warm-ups with Sharon while I answered questions and sorted last-minute things with students, but I found no significant problem to address. Doreen, as always, fixed buttons and switched pants on some Lost Boys, but otherwise, the chaos proved manageable. The kids arranged themselves in a semi-circle, filling the whole stage. They worked breathing, scales, and some rhythmic exercises before concluding with my favorite exercise, "There Is More Love," a simple melody, as Kris explained, "that the students quickly memorize. We use it at the end of the warm-up to allow the students to create and improvise. As I call out sections or categories, those students harmonize with the melody being sung or hum by the remainder of the group." Kris often utilizes this piece before a big rehearsal or when the kids needed focusing, and it's a really beautiful way to emerge from the structure of practice to the space of creation.

They are all yours, Mr. Aubuchon, Kris gently said.

Any costume problems? Any backstage problems? I asked. Hearing none, I told the kids to close their eyes and concentrate on their breathing. Similar to when Kris uses "There Is More Love," I try to focus the kids' energy and give them a bit of pep talk—although less pep and more focus—to set the tone for the day. *As you breathe, with your eyes closed, please extend your right hand,* I said, and placed a tin thimble into each sweaty, teenage palm. In the Darling nursery, Wendy gave Peter a thimble when he didn't know the meaning of a kiss; in return, he gave her an acorn, symbolizing not romantic love but the love of friendship.

> "Surely you know what a kiss is?" Wendy asked.
>
> "I shall know when you give it to me," Peter replied stiffly, and not to hurt his feelings she gave him a thimble (34).

I had commented often on the scene during rehearsals, underscoring the message of friendship I tried to cultivate all season. *I believe you can all fly.* I reminded them. *Every one of you—from the tall to the tiny. So let's fly. All of us. Straight on to Neverland.*

We worked the flying parts first with music. The other ensemble students looked awestruck when the first toes lifted from the stage. We ran a few other parts as well but didn't run the entire show. At 2:45 the orchestra arrived and I gave the kids a break to eat, drink, and take care of any problems they had with their costumes.

Overture downbeat at three o'clock, folks, Kris announced to the cast.

I've learned that professional musicians that Kris hires are almost always early. At 2:45 the entire orchestra had already assembled—except for one.

Where's the harp? I asked.

I don't know. Honestly. Kris took out his phone, which stayed in his pocket during rehearsal. He read me a very apologetic email. *It's just car trouble. He'll be here Wednesday.*

I said I'd believe it when I see it. We both laughed. I wasn't mad at Kris, the harp seemed too good to be true, especially since he had to travel two hours from Rhode Island.

All of Oakmont returned to school from vacation on Monday to find not only the Union Jack and skull-and-crossbones in the lobby, but life-sized cardboard cutouts of Captain Hook and Peter Pan also greeted students in the cafeteria for picture taking during lunches. I couldn't generate enough energy within our community for the show. Things had gone well Sunday night with the exception of the missing harpist, but I also had not received a confirmation reply from the bagpiper, even though I had already paid his deposit without arranging the details for Saturday night. I emailed again that morning and received a short response explaining that his mother had passed away unexpectedly and he was in Scotland to bury her.

What are you going to do about that? Kris asked.

Eh. He's not essential, I just wanted to create old world charm.

I liked the idea, actually. Ask Mr. U., he knows people.

Good idea, I said. *What's with these Celtic musicians?*

Don't even start with the harp today, Jeff.

Mr. Uminski stood in the cafeteria, watching the kids snap selfie pictures with Captain Hook and Peter Pan.

I love this, he said to me, pointing at the kids. *Where's Tinker Bell or is that the wrong story?*

Right story, but her Disney cartoon cutout looked a little seductive—just a little weird—so I only go these two.

Good call.

Did you get your picture taken? I asked.

Not yet, he laughed. *I'm waiting for Mrs. Bogosh and Mrs. Miville to go first.*

They were first in line, I said.

Mr. U. knew a bagpiper through his professional contacts with the Massachusetts State Police, and I found a local piper named Todd Bowdridge who agreed to play that weekend. While the episode hardly represented a crisis, it was another headache I neither needed nor wanted. We rehearsed Monday after school without flying to address any last-minute concerns; the day proved both uneventful and long.

Casting an understudy for Peter presented a different challenge from previous productions. To be sure, both Amanda and Mary brought their own talents to the role and it pained me to only offer Mary the matinee show. I wanted them to approach the character of Peter as each girl saw him, and I stressed to Mary as the understudy not to copy Amanda's performance—I wanted Mary to feel free to be the Peter she understood him to be. If I ever have a similar situation in the future, I might split the shows with each lead having the opportunity to perform twice, or as I did in *Evita* in 2019 when, at every performance, Mary played young Eva Duarte in Act I and Amanda played mature Eva Peron in Act II. I often forgot to give both girls equal rehearsal time; in short, we had to do everything twice. This didn't present a problem, just another thing I struggled to remember during rehearsals.

I again sat in seat J9 during the Tuesday night rehearsal when Mary prepared to fly through the nursery window, elegantly scattering pixie dust as she landed soft-footed. She had practiced the movement on Saturday and Sunday: again, as before, the windows "magically" opened, the piano twinkled on cue, but then I heard—no, felt—a scream I will never erase from my mind. It was an accident, in every possible meaning of the word. Mary's mom, Nicole, leaped to the stage from her audience seat before I could get there. Karen, also a first responder in addition to choreographer, stage manager, and stage mom, jumped into action—the moms took instant care of the banged nose, which gushed blood and, thankfully, had not broken—while the men diagnosed the cause of the error and developed a plan to ensure it would never happen again. I raced to the stage but saw that Nicole and Karen kept everything under control. Mary, I think, endured more of a startle than pain. I asked the kids to step into the hall and clear the stage and I had Kris call Mr. Uminski to explain what had happened. Mary didn't need an ambulance, and I'm sure she would have refused one even if called. When she was ready, Mary got back in the harness to prove she could fly.

After Karen checked both the harness and the connection, I asked everyone, all the adults, to give Mary and me the stage. Unlike many drama students, I didn't teach Mary in history class, so I didn't have the quite same rapport with her as I did some of the others. I've appreciated seeing her in local productions of *Meet Me in St. Louis* and *Mamma Mia!* and, as a result, she has diverse experience of many other directors than me. I knew, however, at that moment, I had to coach her without overdoing it. *You've got this,* I said. *I believe in you.* She nodded with a sniffle. Less than a minute later she flew—and landed—perfectly to the wild cheers of her peers. None of us doubted her for a second.

The bleeding looked much scarier than the actual bruise from hitting her nose on the window casing. "She's a pro and the toughest kid I have ever known. We will never forget tonight but that's ok. Life never goes as planned but in this case so grateful that it's not an eye or head injury," Nicole reassured me by email later that night. Nicole took good care of her, kept the swelling down, and had her rest the next morning, but I saw Mary at school by lunchtime determined to keep going. That's not just the kind of actress Mary is—and indeed, she'll find a career in theatre—but that's the kind of kid she is, too. I was reassured of my policy to have parents present when the kids flew that night. To Nicole's credit, for all the stereotypes that accompany a "show mom," she smashes every one of them. Mary enjoys her roll-with-the-punches attitude because of Nicole. Thankfully, we never suffered another bump, and I had survived my worst nightmare.

Kris and I discussed that moment a year later.

What was going through your mind? he asked me.

I thought my career was over.

Really? For that? Kids get hurt much worse on the field.

The stakes felt higher. The flying represented a different risk.

True.

I also knew in those twenty-or-so minutes that I was the only one in charge. Mr. Uminski wasn't there and it wasn't your music program. I was very aware that I needed to lead at that moment, and it was the first time at Oakmont I felt that weight of responsibility. Kids don't usually get hurt on stage.

Kris nodded as he observed: *Yeah, it was all on you, my friend.*

I had a growth spurt myself that night and it left my head aching, with four days to go.

I texted John from home.

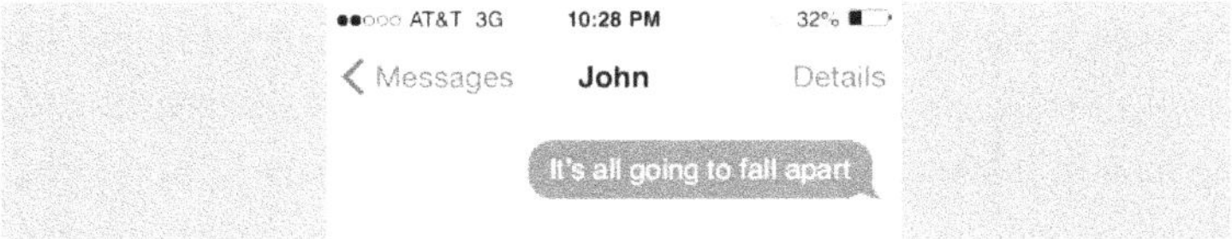

He sent a picture of us in London—his way of saying he believed in me—but no words; he refused to stoke my anxiety.

Act III, Scene 2: Kris

I handed Kris a small package on Wednesday morning as we met in the hall. I acknowledged all my staff with small gifts on opening night, but I tried to find something particularly special for Kris, and I didn't stick around for him to open it. For *Peter Pan*, I gave him a green pocket square embroidered with our "never grow up" logo. I also bought one for my pocket on Saturday night. He's not as sentimental as I am, but the gift became an important milestone in the production season, and it's something I gave extra thought.

Earlier that spring, Dr. Gary Mazzola—Superintendent of Schools for Ashburnham and Westminster—wrote to me and asked if we could accommodate senior citizens, supportive taxpayers in the community, with a special performance like I planned for the children. If not, could I admit the seniors free to a performance? Given the sincerity of his request, I wanted to make it happen, but I knew I lacked a sufficient quantity of tickets. We agreed to allow interested senior citizens to "pop in" to the Wednesday night dress rehearsal, and to make it more special, he offered a spaghetti supper in the school cafeteria hosted by members of the National Honor Society (NHS) who would serve as student ambassadors to the guests.

I stressed to Dr. Mazzola that the fifty or so guests in the audience had to understand we might stop the run if I needed to fix something and he assured me that everyone understood. Although not a "performance" *per se*, this meant a fifth time the kids performed in front of an audience. While everything about the evening exuded positivity, I discontinued the practice for *Evita*, choosing instead to reserve seats in advance for the senior citizens rather than add the pressure of another evening show, even if only for a handful of people.

Dr. Mazzola helped me include another segment of the community to whom I hadn't given particular attention. Welcoming the senior citizens, many of whom had raised children in the towns, was important given their support for the schools over many years. Offering them a night out, and seeing their happy smiles when accompanied by some of Oakmont's finest students, removed a bit of the anxiety that had crept in my thinking on Tuesday night. I asked Dr. Mazzola to reflect on that experience as he neared his retirement in June of 2019. "*Peter Pan* changed the Oakmont community," he wrote, "by serving as a reminder that the true spirit of humankind is to keep kindness in our hearts! This was accomplished by encouraging others to 'reach for the stars' in whatever one does" each day. While the idea and funding for this event should be credited to Dr. Mazzola; Paula Stefanakos, Oakmont English teacher and NHS advisor, orchestrated the evening.

Paula liaised between the Superintendent's office staff and the students to pull everything together for the towns' senior citizens. I asked Paula what she found so meaningful about that night. "Often, elders of a community are called upon to invest in its youth, sort of sight unseen, while the youth of the community do not see the sacrifice of those that were once like them," she wrote. "The magic of that evening shed light on the sacrifice and the investment." Paula's ideas echoed those of a school committee member. I asked Dr. Winifred Kender, who represents Ashburnham, to discuss the senior experience in greater detail. Winnie invested much time in building strong relationships with senior citizens in advance of the NHS dinner which, as she explained, "allowed [the seniors] to hear how motivated, enthusiastic, and kind [the students] were—a sentiment repeated frequently after the event." She explained, however, the show remained the highlight of the experience. "All who attended were impressed with the high quality of the show and said that it gave them hope for the future seeing our youth engaged invaluable activity and working hard, admitting that they often questioned the strength of our younger generation." I had quickly extended invitations to friends at HOPE House, the Beacon of Hope, and the Oakmont Friends Club, but I unintentionally overlooked the senior citizens who, for so many years, had supported both the program and the critical infrastructure that ensures its survival. The initiative of Winnie with Dr. Mazzola and the direction of Mrs. Stefanakos and the National Honor Society became another good lesson of inclusion, by always striving to reach out to all segments of the Ashburnham-Westminster community.

At 6:00, while the senior citizens and NHS members dined in the cafeteria and took selfies with the cardboard Captain Hook and Peter Pan, Kris and I stood in the auditorium reviewing last-minute details when the door opened and in came a six-foot-tall harp pushed, we later saw, by Mason Morton. Kris looked right at me, pointed at my chest, and said, with the widest and most contagious grin imaginable: *the harp is here.*

We couldn't have been more fortunate with Mason. As a member of *Sons of Serendip*, he and the other members of his classical crossover ensemble have made a name for themselves, finishing fourth on the television series *America's Got Talent* in 2014. Beyond that, however, Mason proved himself a gentle, kind, and exemplary musician who worked well with our orchestra and with our kids.

We ran the dress rehearsal as a real performance from warm-ups to bows without interruption. The kids, it turned out, were ready to put on their show. The senior citizens treated it as a real performance, too, clapping loudly to resuscitate Tinker Bell when Peter asked them if they believed, and some even waved goodbye at the finale when Peter and Jane flew back to Neverland. Winnie later wrote to me, "as a senior myself I had to chuckle when one of them told me it made her feel young again and maybe she would start refusing 'to grow up.'" The ticking clock had finally struck midnight—after seventeen months.

It all came together at the dress rehearsal, Kris later said.

I think it was just the addition of the harp, I mused.

Once again, Oakmont "bled green" on Thursday when school filled with hundreds of green "never grow up" t-shirts. Opening night had officially arrived and it promised to start the run in a big way with the special performance for children, paid for by generous community sponsors—that idea I had sleepily hatched the morning after *Grease* closed more than a year before. To allow for early bedtimes, we began the show at 5:00. Some of the kids first had snacks in the cafeteria, so I asked the stage crew to bring the cardboard Hook and Peter for more selfies, and the kids had lots of fun. As I ran back from checking on the festivities in the cafeteria, both Peters—Amanda and Mary—caught me just outside the auditorium.

We know you're very busy, but can we talk? Amanda asked.

My stomach sank into the floor as I feared something dreadful. *Of course. What's up?* They had a box.

We just want to give you this. It's just from us. To thank you.

Guys, I lamented.

Open it, said Mary, smiling.

I did, and as I lifted the lid, I saw the iconic *Eau de Nil* blue of Fortnum & Mason's.

A hamper? You actually got me a Fortnum's hamper? From London?

They nodded. Talk about one of my favorite things!

How did you— I started.

There's something else, Amanda ventured.

I found a well-worn contemporary copy of *Peter Pan* inside.

It has our character notes in the margin. We shared one copy to know what the other was thinking about Peter.

The girls had also inscribed the front cover. I'll keep their comments private, but they each wrote something very similar about growing. For all of Peter Pan's admonition not to grow up, these Peters had, just like I had, and just like we all had.

Thank you. Thank you so much, I repeated. *This means the world to me. Now go get ready,* I said as I shooed them before I turned weepy and they scurried down the hallway, Amanda in green tights and Mary in Mrs. Darling's lovely dress, to get ready for the curtain.

I kept my curtain talk from the ship's deck short and I introduced Mr. Smee just as Mr. Rogers introduced Margaret Hamilton to avoid any scared children. *Max is just a boy, who sits in my class,* I reminded them. Katelyn, an active member of Oakmont Theatre who played a pirate, told me that the swashbuckling entrance of the pirates became her favorite part of the whole show. She found it "so cool to see the reaction of the audience as these 'scary' pirates came out of the doors." Carson, who also played a pirate, echoed Katelyn's words. For her, the brightly colored recorders the pirate band played, which matched their sneakers, made her smile and made the experience of pirating much more humorous than frightening. After introducing Max, I also did something different, I introduced the orchestra—not the musicians, but their instruments. *I want you to listen for their voices in the music, ok?* I said to the children in the audience. *Here's what a harp sounds like.... And here's what trombone sounds like.... And here's the bass—some of you know the bass player, Mr. Lucander—he's the music teacher at one of your schools.*[12] That night, the orchestra didn't play from the pit of the auditorium, they—their instruments—talked with the kids just before the starry lights washed across the dark green curtains, bringing us all to Neverland.

The children delighted in every part of the show, and they "oohed" and "ahhed" in all the right places, especially when Dan and Nick fired the t-shirt cannon at intermission. The kids truly believed in fairies when they fervently clapped their hands to save Tinker Bell. Dan Dufour later explained the impact of the show on his daughter. "Being her first musical experience," he wrote, "the amazing roles of Peter and Smee inspired her to try a role in her class play," a true testament to the power of this experience for the schoolchildren. When I stepped on stage at the end to thank them for coming I saw a sea of boys and girls as well as parents and teachers wearing the eye-patches the pirates had distributed at intermission. Before speaking, I knelt next to Kaden, the fifth-grader who played Michael, and pointed to the whole audience and whispered in his ear, *just remember, tomorrow at school, all those kids saw you fly. For real.* He beamed. As the only member of the cast from an elementary school, Kaden was the hero of Thursday night, and the teenagers—especially his sister Madyson, who played the Lost Girl Nibs—never let him forget it.

Kris saw me with the box as I packed up the auditorium late Thursday night.

Did you tell them about Fortnum's? I asked him.

Huh?

The hamper they gave me. From Fortnum and Mason's?

I don't know what you're talking about right now.

How did they hear about this place in London? I asked, pointing to the label on the box.

Because you tweet everything you do, Jeff. Go get some rest, we have to do this all over again tomorrow.

Ok, ok, I placated.

And do me a favor?

Of course Kris. What?

Eat a vegetable, your gut must be in knots by now.

With that, he disappeared into the shadows of a school hall.

Act III, Scene 3: John & Kris

My breath stopped for a second, the moment had arrived.

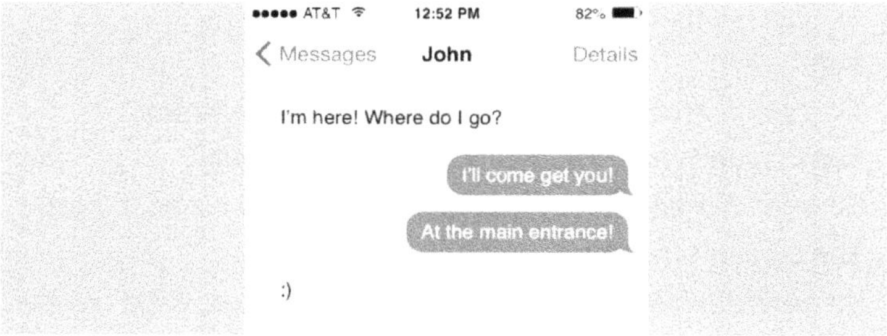

That Friday was cloudy but dry as I popped my head out of the front door of the school. I scanned the parking lot for his black Prius. *He'll be in a rental car,* I remembered. Right before me, John stepped out of a white coupe and adjusted his clothes before turning around.

Hellooo, he said opening his arms. We hugged in the doorway.

Hello old friend. Welcome to my school.

He smiled as we walked into the lobby.

Look at the flags! he noticed.

Wait until you see the ship. We both grinned at the other.

I signed him into the office and made his visit official before heading to my classroom at the rear of the school. Dana watched my A.P. students while they worked through a review of Constitutional Amendments.

You grew up here, he said—a statement not a question.

I did. And I'm still here after all these years.

I'm nostalgic, I haven't been in a high school since I graduated.

What's it like being in a school now? You've never been to Oakmont before.

This part is gorgeous with all this art, but it looks like a labyrinth down there, whoa, he said, pointing down a typically-dark Oakmont hallway.

I showed him the library where I started my Oakmont career and then we turned right to walk down the 300 wing.

This was the Junior High School when I was a student. I had Sex Ed. in that classroom.

Awkward.

Totally awkward. I can't talk to Lincoln in there because of the memories, I said laughing as we passed Four Corners and headed toward classroom 417 at the end of the hall.

As John arrived a few minutes early, I had him join our Constitution review. I introduced him to the class; the drama students had heard stories about John and his career before. My worlds collided with its disparate parts coming together in my classroom. Kris arrived right at 1:00 and after a very brief introduction of my one best friend to the other best friend, Kris whisked John to the band room for his rehearsal with Sharon. *I'll bring him back when we're done,* Kris said, matter-of-factly.

Is he a surprise for us, Mr. A? Max asked after they left.

I don't know what you're talking about, Max. How about we talk about the Twenty-fifth Amendment?

Ok, deal.

Kris and John returned not long after the end-of-school bell.

How'd it go?

Great, Kris said. *All set.*

Good.

I'll see you tonight. 5:30?

Sounds good Kris, thank you.

Thank you, Kris, John said sincerely.

My pleasure, Kris said as he turned back towards his classroom.

Let's go, I said to John. *I need a break from here before tonight. I'll drive.*

I drove to the 110 Grille in Leominster. I had been once or twice before; it's a nice enough place to eat or drink, but not exactly memorable. The conversation centered on the show; to redirect the conversation, I asked about the release of *Faultlines'* new album, but otherwise, we shared nothing ground-breaking. My dry mouth and elevated pulse revealed my anxiousness. For a friendship that easily played out over restaurant tables in California, London, and Massachusetts, that afternoon felt restless. On the one hand, John was just an old friend visiting for a high school play, and yet on the other hand, the evening represented so much more for both of us.

How'd it go with Sharon? I asked for the third or fourth time.

She's such a delight. She's so sweet. It'll be great, relax Jeff.

Kris said she was a little nervous.

She's not the only one.

You're nervous?

Yeah. A little.

Why?

It's a big gig, he laughed.

And you're telling me to relax?

Ha. Yes.

I can't wait. Here, I handed him a small package.

What's this?

A memento, I said, giving him a checkered pocket square. *For your jacket; I have one to match tonight.*

Thank you, he said, folding it and putting it in his breast pocket.

Come on. I've got to go make kids fly.

Kris later told me that, for him, the secrecy surrounding the song made the whole journey so special. I remained totally in the dark as to what would happen that night. I took a piece of paper out of my pocket and handed it to John as we entered the lobby of Oakmont.

Your ticket, I said. *Seat J10.*

Will I see you?

I hope so, I'm sitting in J9.

My to-do list had grown long when we returned at 5:00, especially to set-up the box office and concessions. The Thursday children's show didn't require our typical set-up so on Friday I had tables with tablecloths to arrange, signs to post, and kids to manage. John proved himself a good friend and rolled up his sleeves to help.

I forget this part of your job, he said. *I'm spoiled as a performer.*

I'm sure Andrew Lloyd Webber doesn't move tables before Evita opens, I said. Our eyes again met across the table we moved, causing us both to laugh.

Kris, Karen, Doreen, and Mike arrived at 5:30, and warm-ups began promptly at 6:00. The hustle of the afternoon probably overwhelmed John. Matt Bourgault and his team from AWCA-TV finalized their filming arrangements while

Kris and I finished putting things in order. If we had buzzed on Thursday afternoon, we swarmed on Friday.

Here's J10, I said. *Have a seat while I help the kids. Listen to the harp warm up.*

Sounds good, he smiled, taking it all in.

I love Billy Wilder's *Sunset Boulevard*. In fact, Jenn and I took the Paramount Studios tour in Los Angeles once and saw Stage 18 where Norma Desmond made her Hollywood comeback. In the film, as in the musical, the people, sets, and activity all mesmerize Norma; she remembers loving the movie set as if she "never said goodbye." Twice I saw Glenn Close perform that role on Broadway, and I often recall Norma's apprehension, anticipation, and my own love of the stage in the moments before a show. John watched all that unfold that evening—both the activity as well as my love for it—from seat J10.

Kris began warm-ups at 6:00 and I invited John to join the kids on stage.

Really?

You need to warm up, don't you? This is your chance to learn from the maestro.

Good point, he nodded, with a bit of apprehension.

They know you're my best friend, that's why they think you're here, I said. *They have no idea.*

When the kids and John had concluded "There Is More Love," I asked them, as always, to focus on their breathing. I try to give a different reflection before each performance, and that afternoon I focused on friendship, both for them as individuals and for us collectively as a cast. I made no specific mention of

John, but most of them probably understood why I emphasized friendship that evening. I appreciated seeing the circle of my students standing shoulder to shoulder on stage with John among them. Never could I have imagined the scene a year before, when I nervously sat at a table at his gig in Beverly Hills. I knew true love then.

I'm proud of you all, I said while looking at John. *His eyes were closed but he smiled. And I believe you can fly. Every one of you. So again, let's fly to Neverland.*

The kids scattered as the doors opened at 6:30, sharp.

I need to go get ready, I told John. *Just sit and relax. Introduce yourself when my parents arrive, they're sitting next to you.*

It's true, we've never met in all these years, he grinned.

The Caouettes will sit across the aisle. Say hi to them, too; everyone knows who you are, I said, nudging his arm. *I've bragged plenty.*

I dressed in my tuxedo in the faculty bathroom with a long green tie and vest for Friday. My checkered pocket square matched John's. I looked in the mirror. *You're old for 37, almost 38,* I said to the mirror. *It's the salt and pepper hair. It's got to go.* I stepped into the hallway to a chorus of "ooohs," with only five minutes until curtain.

Why the tux, Mr. A? Asked a tall Lost Boy named James.

Because you're that special. Are you ready, Mr. DeMoura?

It's a full house out there, Kris said.

It was full a month ago, I grinned.

I took a final quick walk backstage and checked with Karen and Doreen to make sure everyone was ready. The clock on my phone said 6:58.

Are you nervous? Kris asked.

The show was great last night, they've got this.

Are you nervous about the end? He spoke vaguely with the kids standing nearby.

I gently nodded yes.

Seven o'clock, he said.

I know of only one unbroken tradition that Kris and I developed on the opening night of *The Sound of Music*: we always hugged before we entered the auditorium together at the start of a performance. Neither of us planned it, and now I can't imagine starting a show differently.

Again from the poop-deck, I welcomed the audience, thanked Mr. Lantry and his students for the flame-retardant ship, and explained that all four auditorium emergency exits remained clear and in working order. I also hinted at the intermission fun: cannon fire and a live auction. Just after my teary dedication to the memory of Mr. Samuel DeMoura, I concluded my talk by saying, *And now Mr. DeMoura, let's fly to Neverland.* Cue the applause, starry lights, woodwind trills, and, of course, a harp glissando as I walked up the dark aisle to seat J9. I waved to my friends the Caouettes who sat in J6, J7, and J8, as well as mom and dad who sat in J11 and J12. I again nudged John in the arm as I took my seat while the orchestra played through the *Overture*. Knowing that I could no longer ensure a perfect performance, I watched the reactions of the nearby people for whom I cared so much.

I turned to John when the lights came up at intermission.

Jeff, he said with emphasis, his eyes widening with the lights.

Do you like it?

So good.

Thanks, friend. I smiled.

They're literally a tough act to follow.

You'll do great. We're far from Beverly Hills here.

Believe me, I know.

I squeezed his arm as I greeted my parents and then the Caouettes before heading backstage to encourage the kids.

I handed a framed and signed cast poster to Captain Hook because I needed his help on the ship. For the last few years, I auctioned just three such posters during performance intermissions and they fetched several hundred dollars each.[13] With the budget for *Peter Pan* hovering around $30,000, I needed to find every possible penny. *You're bidding not just on a poster,* I said, *but you're making the dream of flying a reality for our students. So please bid high.* I started with $50 and quickly got to $250, where the bid stalled a little and I had to energize the crowd. *It takes a lot of meatballs and pancakes to make these kids fly,* I said (year after year, the crowd always laughed at that one). We soon reached $450 and I remember from $450 to $650 it became a bidding war between the father of one of the Peters and a man I didn't recognize but who sat in H9, just in front of John. It appeared he bid for a woman with white hair seated next to him—and I realized for whom. I looked for Kris with the orchestra but I couldn't locate him in the pit. *Will someone please find Mr. DeMoura and have him get in here, soon?* I asked into the microphone. His mother pushed the bid higher and higher, to the astonishment and genuine delight of everyone. Kris walked onto the floor from the ship as the bid hit $750—from Peter's dad. Mrs. DeMoura whispered to his son who said, firmly:

One thousand dollars.

SOLD! I yelled with uproarious applause. *To Mrs. Jean*

DeMoura of Florida!

Kris walked up the aisle to his brother Kenny and mother. The three of them embraced as the audience stood and cheered.

Our school is special not because we have generous benefactors, but because we are family here—both biological and adopted, I said as Hook brought the poster to the DeMouras, and today it hangs in Kris's office.

The DeMoura family.

About a month before *Evita* opened in 2019, I searched through old photographs from *Peter Pan.* Like the green "never grow up" pocket square I gave to Kris in 2018, I needed another special gift for the opening night of *Evita.* With help from Sue O'Connor, a cast mom and a professional photographer, I gave Kris this framed photograph for his opening night gift in 2019. It's now the companion to the signed cast poster his proud mother gave him. Sue also gave me one of these framed photos, which sits with other pictures of my family because my "family" includes the DeMouras.

Between the amazement on your face, and that she had given as much as she did, the whole moment left me astonished as I sat right behind her, John told me a year later at a Hollywood chicken restaurant called *The Birds.* He spoke the truth; the episode had lasted less than five minutes, but left us all awestruck and humble, in turn ratcheting the suspense for Friday night's finale.

The kids received another standing ovation (they were three for three by now) and again I took to the stage. *We often give flowers here at Oakmont to recognize student achievement in the performing arts. I did last year, and I'm sure I will again; but this year,* I said, turning to the assembled cast on stage, *I wanted to give you something personal. Something special. Something that you'll never get again in your life and you'll remember was created just for you. Like a song. And I happen to know a rather talented singer and songwriter.* I heard slight gasps from the kids behind me. *So all the way from sunny Hollywood, my dear friend John Flanagan is here with a song that he wrote—and I've not yet heard—just for you.*

A mix of awws and applause rumbled as John walked on stage from J10. Karen brought out a stool for me to sit on; we had prearranged this, not knowing exactly how tired I'd be or how the song would affect me. John and I hugged as I handed him the microphone and he introduced his song with very few words. With the entire cast arrayed behind and around us in costume, Kris gently gave Sharon the tempo and she played a new melody that sounded, if you can imagine, just like twinkling stars.

How do I count the stars?
And how will I know,
the second from a thousand other ones?
I don't know where we are
All I know is that I trust
Somewhere there is a place for us.

'Cause we are only lost boys and lost girls
searching for a home in a lonely world.
Shadows and firelight, fighting for a place in the night.
If we close our eyes and try,
maybe just one time,
We can fly...

Blame it on innocence.
I gave you a thimble when,
really what you needed was a kiss
Easier to pretend, I guess
So I dig my heels into the mud
And promise myself, I'm never growing up.

'Cause we are only lost boys and lost girls
searching for a home in a lonely world.
Shadows and firelight, fighting for a place in the night.

If we close our eyes and try,
maybe just one time,
We can fly...

Darling, leave a light on for me
So I can fall asleep.

John Flanagan and the premier of his original song, "Fly."

John reminded the whole school we can fly—the very lesson I had tried to teach for a year. When I watch the recording of that moment, I like to look at the kids' expressions. At first, they don't know what to make of him, but their eyes and smiles widen at the start of the second verse when, as he often does, shows the heights his upper vocal range by climbing the tenor scale. Kris's wife, Jenn, later told me that she was similarly moved watching the faces of the students and audience "by this original song from a California songwriter who cared so much about our kids without ever having met them." For me, the three-and-a-half minutes couldn't have been more perfect: he nailed the melody, the words, and the idea. I sat there contentedly, knowing I had given *Peter Pan*—and, more importantly, my students and the community who had helped me grow up as a boy—everything I could. In hearing the song, I think the kids and their parents came to understand that, too. John certainly had.

The late night stars twinkled by the time we drove back to my house for dinner. There's little open after 10:00 pm in central Massachusetts that's not part of a fast-food chain. My sister had cleaned my house from top to bottom that day as her opening night gift to me. She had also picked up and arranged a very healthy and simple, gluten-free meal that my aunt had prepared for us, knowing I would be far too tired to cook anything. Both Jenn and my aunt Cathy reminded me of the many ways people supported the project and me. John and I sat at my table, toasted with champagne in new blue flutes, ate, laughed, and remembered the performance. I planned to return to California in two weeks for another *Faultlines* show. Our visits had become more frequent than they had ever been; our friendship felt stronger than ever. Time had healed the rocky ending to our London weekend and peace enveloped my little townhouse that night. After dinner, we sat on the couch together, both exhausted from the week.

Why did you do it? I asked.

You asked.

I ask for lots of things.

This has all been so important to you for so long. I knew it at the

Peter Pan statue in London, too.

Thanks, friend.

I don't usually write solo. This pushed me to grow a little bit this year. Maybe a lot.

He fidgeted with his phone a bit while I rested my eyes until I recognized the same piano melody Sharon played a few hours before. He softly sang "Fly" for me—just me this time—with that worn 1911 copy of *Peter and Wendy* he had given me years earlier on the bookshelf next to us, my head rested on his shoulder, nearly asleep.

I have an early flight, with an L.A. gig tomorrow. Let's clean up, he said, helping me stand.

No, I'll do the dishes tomorrow, it's too late, I said as I walked him to the door.

Thank you, friend, he said, embracing me.

Thank you, John. I'll see you in two weeks.

He walked to his car, alone, in the dark. Like my grandfather, I waited until he drove away before turning out the porch light. "Second star to the right and straight on till morning," I remembered Peter Pan saying, similarly gazing at the night sky from the Darling window.

Act III, Scene 4: Jeff

I woke Saturday morning content but sleepy. I didn't leap from my bed, but when I had my coffee, I set to washing the few dishes from the night before. I looked at the round, glass dining room table set for two, with new blue-colored things and champagne flutes to celebrate the evening. I smiled; it really had been everything I had hoped for. My sister had left the rest of the house spotless along with a brown paper package for me; I unwrapped the package to find an old Vermont barn board into which she had beautifully scorched the word *Neverland.* The board was shaped like an arrow, like the kind you find in Kensington Gardens pointing you to the Peter Pan statue. She left a note, "made from an old ship's board, found by some lost boys." I treasure little more as much as that gift.

I brought my tuxedo jacket and pants to the cleaners to have them pressed for the Saturday evening show. I drove to Starbucks while I waited for the pressing then picked up my clothes and headed to school. The theatre moms—Megan, Patti, and Kim—would arrive soon to prepare lunch for the HOPE House and Beacon of Hope guests. Their daughters had all been in *Grease* and the lunch served as a reunion for them, and what a gift they gave to their neighbors in the community! They prepared large servings of hot macaroni and cheese as well as smaller sandwiches for the HOPE House kids, and a large deli platter of sandwiches for the guests from the Beacon of Hope. Mimi, home now from France, would handle the crowd and, she later told me, eagerly awaited seeing the HOPE House kids.

I arrived at school around 10:30 to put in an hour's work before the moms arrived. When I turned the key and stepped into room 417, fumbling with the hangers that held my tux, I saw some small sheets of paper on my bare wooden desk. I gently set down the things from my hands to pick up the papers—John's handwritten lyrics and chords to *Fly*. No note, nothing sentimental, just the words in his own handwriting. I remember I still held my keys and, as I looked at the sheets of paper, put my key-ring in my pocket. I sensed something irregular as I continued to read the lyrics. *No wallet,* I realized as I checked all my pockets, I always keep my wallet in my front right pocket. *Nothing.* Panic set in as I raced to the front of the building to search my car. *No. It's not here. Must be at the cleaners. Must be. I paid her.* Sitting in the driver's seat of my parked Jeep, I Googled the cleaners and called. The line buzzed. I tried again. *Did you find a wallet?* I blurted instead of saying hello.

Hello, she said.

Did you find a wallet?

A wallet? Yes. It is here.

I'll be right there. I now had to fit an hour's errand into fifty minutes. I called Kris.

Hey, he said, sounding calm and relaxed as usual.

Hey, what time are you getting to school?

I thought you said noon?

Yes, but, can you get here early? I lost my wallet and someone needs to be there at 11:30 to help the moms with lunch. I think the flyers wanted to practice with Mary, too.

I'll do my best. It should be close.

Thanks, Kris.

You got it. Where are the harnesses?

Locked in the closet, so only you or I can get them for the parents.

Good.

When I returned to the cleaners, the kind woman retrieved my wallet from her desk.

A man found it, outside. She pointed.

Thank you so much, I said as I turned and walked back to my Jeep. I checked the contents: license and credit cards, but no cash. About $100 was missing. *No time to stress about that now,* I reassured myself as I headed back to school, the rare time I passed Starbucks without stopping.

I got a text just as I parked in the front of school. I took Mr. Uminski's spot since it was Saturday.

I saw Mimi's shadow against the light that poured through the

Four Corners skylight. We hugged, but I wasn't as composed as I had wanted to be at that moment. The missing wallet derailed my morning and the cast would arrive soon, with the first lunch guests at 12:30. The HOPE House lunch had been one of the first big ideas I had for the matinee—well, Mimi's idea—and I wanted it to be a great success. I worried that, in my haste, things would fall apart.

How's the show going? Mimi asked excitedly.

It's good. Today's been crazy.

Don't stress, we'll take care of all of this, Jeff. Trust me.

In my classroom, I had a cart loaded with the things she needed: mostly water bottles but also table cloths and cutlery. Mimi wheeled it down to the cafeteria.

What's it like being back in school?

Weird Jeff. So weird.

You're not in Paris anymore.

Hell no.

Tell your mom I'll be there after I sort out the auditorium.

We've got it, Jeff. It's ok. Détends-toi!

Thank you, Mimi. I stopped walking in order to be authentic.

Of course, Jeff, she laughed. *Cha-Cha wasn't going to miss it. Honest.*

I had to compose myself as I walked into the auditorium. The flyers wanted to practice early with Mary to ease everyone's nerves, but especially hers. Amanda flew during the previous nights' shows without incident and I knew everything would go just as well with Mary. I unlocked the storage closet so that Karen could fit Mary into her harness. I don't remember saying anything out of the ordinary to Mary, I knew everything would be fine, and it was; in fact, her stellar matinee performance warranted applause that she would hopefully remember for years to come. I burst with real joy for her.

I popped into the cafeteria to find everything under control—those three moms ran a ship tighter than Admiral Lantry. Mimi met the HOPE House bus that had been paid for by the NHS students and reconnected with many of her old program friends. The moms bustled about welcoming everyone while their husbands did a fair amount of logistical work behind the scenes. The kids ate quickly, however. I'm not sure who had the good idea, but Mimi took the HOPE kids outside in the beautiful April weather for some on-the-spot games. As I bustled through the lobby at 1:45 to ensure an on-time curtain, I saw Mimi, giving some small tyke a piggy-back ride down the hall, trailed by her own company of Lost Boys and Girls. How glad I was not only that she came, but that, in the end, she and her family, were so instrumental in helping the HOPE House kids on their journey to Neverland.

At intermission, I turned to my grandfather and asked, *how do you like the finished ship?*

Boy, is it something, he said, shaking his head. I smiled.

I also found two old friends—Benedictine monks in layman's clothes from my *alma mater*, Saint Anselm College. Not just monks, actually; Abbot Mark Cooper is Chancellor of the College and Father Augustine Kelly served as Dean of the College when I taught there a decade earlier.

This is fantastic, said Father Augustine encouragingly as he hugged me. *This is like collegiate theatre.*

Captain Hook is phenomenal, Abbot Mark said. *Is he a student?*

He is, I assured. *In fact, he's a senior here now and next year, he'll be with you at Saint Anselm. Two of the girls playing braves with Tiger Lily are also going to Saint A's, Hannah and Isabel.*

You're joking, Father Augustine said.

I'm really proud of them all. James, especially, was born an Anselmian. I said.

What will he study? Father Augustine asked.

Political science. I said. *He'll do well.*

That's wonderful. Father Augustine elated.

Stick around after the bows, I'll introduce him to you, it'll mean a lot to him.

We will. Good job, Jeffrey, Abbot Mark said with his hand on my shoulder, making me blush. The chancellor of my college had not only found the time to attend the show but seemed proud of me. As promised, I brought James right to Abbot Mark and Father Augustine at the end of the show. They congratulated him and looked forward to seeing him on the New Hampshire hilltop in the fall.

After the bows of the Friday and Saturday shows, I invited Jasmine Goodfellow on stage to share her prepared comments with the cast and audience. She delivered her words calmly and gently. In handing the microphone to Jasmine, I acknowledged on behalf of Oakmont—rather than ignored—the problems inherent in Barrie's play. Jasmine reiterated what the group had believed all along: that Barrie, like most Anglo-American men in 1904, misunderstood and mischaracterized Native Americans; but in creating Neverland, he celebrated good things like childhood innocence, friendship, and bravery. I was, however, most moved by this idea from Jasmine's brief talk: *I don't want to hate this play,* she said with sixty or so costumed teenagers standing on stage behind her. *Thanks to Oakmont, I don't.* From that July afternoon in Starbucks with Kris, when I first hatched the idea, throughout all the heated exchanges of email, the meetings, collaborations, and explanations of the work, Jasmine—without any input from me—had captured the essence of what Karen choreographed: to celebrate, in a spirit of friendship, the enduring lessons in *Peter Pan* while acknowledging that today's values thankfully differ from those of 1904. While the project was imperfect, I think we came close to our ideal while remaining faithful to the script and story. The students and community shared this consensus in the afternoon discussion.

I never tired of watching Dana teach. I rarely got the chance to observe him—often only as I passed by his classroom and listened to his instruction. Dana studied both sides of the stereotyping issue at length when we gathered to discuss it on Saturday afternoon. While the forum audience mostly filled with history students compelled to participate by extra credit, some community members stayed along with Bob Goodby, James Stanley, and Tammy Bucchino. The discussion proved mild. Those who stayed supported, rather than criticized, the program. Still, we offered a forum for dialog. The participating cast members repeatedly said things like *we learned so much*, or, *we discovered another viewpoint*, just as Lauren wrote in her earlier email. In those moments when the Humanities project became most trying, Kris always brought me back to the same question: *what's in the best educational interest for our students?* In listening to the dialogue that afternoon, I am confident we achieved our goal.

After forty-five minutes, Dana concluded the thoughtful discussion and informal groups continued to talk in the aisles. Daniella Zalcman interviewed a few of the older girls among Tiger Lily's braves, although Oakmont was never mentioned in her article the following December. The discussions expressed nothing but positivity; I was happy for the interviewed kids and felt my eyelids grow heavy while my head pounded from dehydration. *Just six more hours,* I reminded myself.

In the cafeteria, the rest of the cast relaxed and ate their pizza, expertly organized by a parent—Kim Tabor—every year, reminding me how the families of Oakmont Theatre truly came together to make the productions such a success. Brittany Smeltekop had delivered two giant sheet cakes for the cast, courtesy of the Friends Club, in gratitude for their complimentary tickets to the Friday night show. In the relative calm, I saw Kris sitting with Sharon and Karen; I joined them.

You ok? Kris asked.

Yeah. Wiped.

You look it, Karen said.

I've got to go count the matinee money and deposit it in the safe.

Eat first, Jeff. Eat. And drink, you look flush. It's all so wonderful. Sharon never fails to be kind.

Sounds good, I said. *Does anyone have an antacid?*

Sharon immediately opened her purse and maternally searched for something to relieve my indigestion.

Finale

You made my day stressful, I said to the tux as I stepped into the pants for the last time. I snapped a selfie in the mirror to show John the snow-white bowtie and vest for the finale. I sent it by text with a bit of encouragement for him:

The message delivered but he didn't respond. I finished putting my street clothes away and steeled myself for the finale. *He's tired,* I guessed. *And busy with his gig tonight back in L.A. It was good of him to come last night. Still, it's the finale.*

This is it, Kris said as I stepped into the hall. *The end of the flight.*

Next year's an adventure, too. Has the orchestra learned the title music for the big reveal?

Yes, we practiced it this afternoon. Next year won't be as big as this, will it?

God, no. I'll die.

The house is full, Jeff.

The house is packed. Let's spy through the portholes.

Admiral Lantry had cut two authentic-looking portholes into the side of the ship and provided a bench on which to stand. I'm not sure if anyone noticed Kris and I looking through the windows, but we saw everyone even without a spyglass.

Everyone is here Kris, have you ever seen this many faculty retirees at a show?—it's everyone, Kris. Everyone has come out for Dave and June.

Everyone except the bagpiper, where the hell is he? I heard him playing in the lobby.

I know, he's supposed to come in here before we go on, he's two minutes late.

Two minutes? Chill, Jeff. It's almost over. Try to enjoy it.

Kris' timing was impeccable as the auditorium door opposite opened and in stepped the bagpiper in kilt and coat playing *Scotland the Brave.*

Fitting for Mr. Barrie, don't you think? I beamed.

The piper stepped onto the stage while playing and marching in place before exiting through the main doors. He had set the mood and the time had come to touch the stars one last time.

Perfect timing, I said.

Just like the harp. Break a leg, my friend.

You, too, Kris.

We hugged a moment longer than normal—I remembered his dad—and then I took an extra deep breath before climbing the stairs of the ship and stepped into the lights.

Tonight is a special night, Oakmont, I said standing aboard Admiral Lantry's *BAS2018. You'll notice the banner on stage with words of thanks to Mr. and Mrs. Lantry, who are the reason why so many of us are here tonight. The banner is simple in its truth: Mr. and Mrs. Lantry do believe every one of us at Oakmont flies, every day.* The audience delightfully interrupted me with their applause. *And next to the banner, a wooden rocking horse to remind us of the Darling nursery, where our story begins. Mr. Lantry lovingly carved that rocking horse for his daughters some thirty years ago. Those three girls are here tonight with their own children to celebrate their grandparents. How special our Oakmont family is because of them.* Quite naturally, and without prompt, 480 people stood to applaud these educators who had given their careers to the school, manifest in the epic ship on which I stood. Dave and June stood and embraced as the cavernous auditorium filled with applause and, more importantly, love. *And now, Mr. DeMoura, one last time,* my voice cracked as I made eye contact with Kris, *let's all fly to Neverland.* The applause continued and overpowered the *Overture*, including the (expensive) harp.

Of all the things I remember about the Saturday night show, I most cherish the audience's applause when the Darling children flew. Of course, the audience adumbrated the moment—many of the parents had been to all the previous shows—but when the four kids took to the air and moved through the night sky, the audience cheered in a way they had not before. For the many times I had tweeted #WeAllFly that season, the kids soared the highest on Saturday night. Similarly, the resuscitation of Tinker Bell at the end of Act II brought the entire audience together in a moment of shared belief. I can't imagine a curmudgeon sat in that auditorium who didn't believe in fairies that night, and if they did, he kept silent about it.

Jefé! My old nickname rang across the lobby at intermission.

Only one person—Mr. John Blackwell—could have remembered it. He looked the same and spread the same joy and enthusiasm as always. I was never a great musician, and not ever one of his best music students, but I'm proud to have held the director's job he once did. He told me, shaking my hand there in the lobby, that he was just as proud of me to have it. "A job well done, keep up the great work—JB" he later wrote to Kris and me. When I climbed aboard the *Jolly Roger* to provide the intermission entertainment, I prefaced the fun by saying, *We have a special guest in the audience, ladies and gentlemen. The director of eighteen Oakmont musicals across his thirty-five-year career, Mr. John Blackwell is here with us tonight with his wife Ellen.* The community applauded them and seemed to appreciate having the Blackwells back with us. His affirmation after those eighteen years away made me very happy.

The live auction again brought much enthusiasm but didn't fetch the $1000 Mrs. DeMoura had so generously given the program the night before. Something happened, however, as I descended the darkened stairs to my seat for the remainder of Act III. From time to time, I have an irregular heartbeat—most frequently in times of fatigue or stress—and it's triggered by taking a wrong step or standing too quickly. I've told the doctors, but I've never been able to recreate it for them. They've all said I'll be fine and, ironically, not to stress about it. I did, however, have an episode of tachycardia that night. I managed to get back to my seat, but it was a bad spell. I perspired through my collar, in fact, I used the embroidered pocket square identical to the one I gave Kris and, evidently, the silk bled because it left a trace of blue around my mouth and on my neck where I kept wiping the sweat away. I tried what a doctor once explained to me as the Valsalva maneuver, which usually ends the spell, but this time did not. I closed my eyes to breathe deeply; it didn't help and I couldn't breathe enough air. The pounding in my chest persisted, to the point where I imagined those sitting nearby could feel it, never mind hear it. I didn't dare stand, I feared a heart attack and thought, quite honestly, I would leave school in an ambulance. I don't remember when it ended or how, but like a magician's spell, it broke and I could breathe again. I've had an irregular heartbeat since then, but never one as bad or as scary. I'm pretty sure my body told me—no urged me—that I had done enough and the time had come to rest. Only one more set of bows, and one last farewell, remained.

When I choose a show to direct, I imagine a single scene and the rest of the production scaffolds from that one idea. The task isn't just to translate the script to the stage; rather, as Kris always says, to make it ours. As I block that primary scene, a faint image from my mind comes to life on stage, usually in a big company number, as a powerful creative moment to bring us all—cast, crew, and audience—together. In *The Sound of Music*, the finale and reprise to "Climb Ev'ry Mountain" featured all the students, both nuns and Nazis, together holding hands. They were, after all, high school friends and not belligerents. In both *Grease* and *Evita,* the cast danced in and with the audience at the end of Act I with "We Go Together" and "A New Argentina." While my initial fascination with Peter Pan stemmed from his flight across the London skyline, my imagination always returned to Peter's ballad "Neverland," both in Act I and at the finale. While the script calls for just Peter and Jane at the finale, I brought all sixty-five actors on stage to wave goodbye as Peter flew back to Neverland with tiny Jane. I did not, however, anticipate the power of that initial, foreshadowed scene in the nursery.

In the nursery, early in Act I, Peter says he must not ever be touched and so I used the arc of that song to build trust between Peter and Wendy and to have Wendy take Peter's hand as they walked downstage from the window, with Peter singing:

So come with me where dreams are born,
and time is never planned.
Just think of lovely things,
and your heart will fly on wings,
Forever, in Never Neverland.

The girls who played Peter, Amanda and Mary, both earned immeasurable applause each time they sang that last verse and I used that powerful moment for a post-bow reprise. I also invited the audience to sing that reprise with us. At the performance for senior citizens, brave grandmothers waved back as the cast sang their goodbyes in a moment of true beauty. While most of the audiences sang perfunctorily, the Saturday evening audience—still on their feet from an epic standing ovation—sang with gusto: picture more than 500 voices from our community singing that verse together with a full orchestra (and harp): *Forever, in Never Neverland!* In fact, the voices again overpowered the professional musicians. In a creative journey that always sought belonging and inclusion, we seemed to find it—even if only for a solitary moment—at the grand finale. I learned that Oakmont Theatre was important to me because I also wanted to be included among those creative souls—adults and students—making the work of inclusion all the more meaningful.

We stood together, some 480 people in the audience, with sixty-five kids holding hands on stage after the bows, and helpers all around, singing one last time: *Forever, in Never Neverland!* At the other shows, some sang enthusiastically while others fell silent; but something magical happened at the finale, just like when the audience clapped the first time the kids took to the air—and again to save Tinker Bell—everyone seemed to believe, and everyone, I hope, felt included. Our work had drawn to a close, but before I approached the stage to thank so many people and reveal the 2019 show, I'd pass Dave and June Lantry—I'd smile to see Dave holding his grandson—before I passed Mimi and Maura (I hugged them both as the chorus reached the last "Neverland") and I stepped up the stairs to the continued applause for the kids. But before all that, before I even left my seat, I squeezed the hand of the person sitting next to me in seat J10: my sister. Jenn stood with me at the grand finale just as she stood with me along the chilly Thames in London two Decembers before, watching Peter Pan leap across the great clock face. Our completed journey started almost eighteen months earlier, on another Saturday night, under another starry sky, so far from home.

I climbed the stairs while the audience continued to cheer wildly for the kids. As I stepped into the lights, the radiating cast—as if cued—all took a step backward, making way for me to cross. I shook hands, patted backs, and hugged outstretched arms as I made my way to center stage. I choked when I turned to face the audience and found them still clapping. There, in the darkness, I faintly saw retired teachers who had come to celebrate Dave and June and their ship, my colleagues whom I counted among my dearest friends, former students like Mimi and Maura, and loved ones who had traveled far. I'm not certain how long the moment lasted, but I savored it. I thanked the kids, the parents, and all the adults who had truly helped our kids soar, especially Karen, Doreen, Sharon, and Kris. The flight reached its end, the clock had finally wound down, and rather than weep, the time arrived to find another far-off place to travel. Karen brought on stage a cardboard tube, which I in turn handed to the club president, Mia, to open just as I had handed a box to Maura at the end of *Grease* a year before. As the first bit of pale blue cloth of the flag emerged from the tube, the orchestra burst into "Don't Cry for Me Argentina," to the clear delight and applause of the audience.

Mike Parenteau began to sweep the auditorium as the last guests departed and I caught up with Kris in the pit while Mason packed his harp.

Good show, my friend, I said embracing him and fighting tears.

It was a good show. Really great. You look exhausted.

I am. In every possible way.

You've got a whole summer to rest, Jeff, make sure you do. Have you considered a trip to Maine?

Eh. You and I have that brunch tomorrow that Mrs. Uminski is hosting. Then I have to pack the ropes with the parents and then it's onto the next. You know, one show bleeds into the other.

It's a shame there's no harp in next year's show, he pointed discreetly to Mason. *He's great.*

I know. I already read the orchestration.

Can we use a harp? I'll book him tonight.

No, we need an accordion. You've got eleven months. Now we need that old world sound for Buenos Aires.

An accordion, dear Lord. Kris laughed as he looked toward the rafters. *See you tomorrow.* He patted my back and turned to walk up the aisle, leaving the score to *Peter Pan* on his music stand. I sat down in J9 in the almost-empty auditorium; Mike continued to sweep and I looked at the ship.

Great job, Boss. Those kids really flew, Mike called from across the auditorium, propping himself up on his broom. *But it's time to lock up, brother.*

Yup. It's been a long, long week Mikey, I said, wiping my eyes.

He gave me a thumbs-up before he said: *I'll get the lights.*

When I arrived at school on Sunday, Keith Aubin had taken command of the apparatus disassembly. The kids would strike the rest of the set on Monday, but Keith and his team quickly packed the heavy equipment and folding the backdrops. I felt superfluous and had plenty of other things to count, pack away, and sort. With so many hands, the work wrapped-up in a short time and I wheeled the heavy crate down to the delivery door, ready for collection on Monday. I affixed the shipping labels as instructed and brushed my hand over the lid—almost like saying goodbye to a friend in a closed coffin. *I never got to fly*, I thought, turning and walking back down the silent hallway in the empty school.

A paper Dunkin' Donuts bag waited for me on my desk Monday morning with a note: *May your memories of this week be as sweet as the treat inside. Katie.* In many ways, Katie Miville and I couldn't be more different: where she's sporty I'm theatrical; where she teaches math I teach letters. I remember the first time I met her, early in 2011 when I returned to Oakmont, she introduced herself and invited me out for a drink with some of the other teachers. She's thoughtful when it matters most and excellent in her new role as Assistant Principal. That donut brought me as much joy and gratitude as her social invitation years earlier. I caught up with her later in the day and asked how she liked the show, and I watched her quickly grow nervous.

Ok, you see, a mom came into school Thursday and needed tickets and we just didn't have any, so I gave her mine. I figured it was more important for her to see the show than me, it's on DVD right?

Of course, Katie. You're thoughtful and welcoming to the last. Thank you.

The ship disappeared entirely on Monday, as eerily as it had arrived. Theatre is like a ghost—to paraphrase Maggie Smith—one moment it's there, and then it's gone. Mr. Lantry's engineering students dismantled it and salvaged almost everything.

What are you going to do with all that material? I asked Admiral Lantry on Tuesday.

Save the steel for when you need it next.

Good. What about the wood sheathing—that was good flame-retardant stuff.

Buddy benches.

Say again?

The kids are making buddy benches next fall in Wood Tech.

What's a buddy bench?

The clue is in the name. It's a bench. You sit with a buddy, Jeff.

Got it.

Don't you teach A.P.? Keep up. Dave smiled as he said it.

Whose brilliant idea was that?

Brittany, of course.

Brittany Smeltekop is brilliant, but the idea was neither hers nor does she take credit for it. Google "buddy bench" to learn more. The benches became Dave's final—and unexpected—gift to Oakmont and the community. Two of the benches now sit in the elementary schools and one remains in Oakmont at Four Corners. I asked Brittany about them.

It's a social opportunity, she said. *When Kyle* [one of the members of the Friends Club] *is on the bench, the bench is full. I love that it is made from repurposed materials from Peter Pan.* She continued to emphasize the collaborative nature of the project, how the donated wood came out of an idea for *Peter Pan*, and the students turned the wood into benches, and now one bench sits at Four Corners. *I loved that so many of my special education students were able to be a part of that journey,* she finished.

Walking past the bench, you could never imagine it once crashed through the auditorium walls as a pirate ship—where Peter Pan and Captain Hook dueled, and the innocence of youth triumphed over the hubris of adulthood. Soon enough, the "wood techers" who built the benches and the ship will have graduated. Undoubtedly, they will tell their own kids someday how they built a real pirate ship in school, but I don't imagine they will remember the bench as much. Yet, as this journey heralded inclusion and friendship, how beautiful it is that the only lasting artifact from *Peter Pan* purposefully brings kids together. Day after day, whether it's Kyle or someone else, kids—as well as teachers with kids—sit on that bench built by Mr. Lantry and his students—to navigate the rough waters of growing up.

A buddy bench, built from the ship timbers. Notice the "B."

I saw James—Captain Hook—in the corridor later that week wearing a sweatshirt from Saint Anselm College. For all his humor on stage, and talent in Kris' ensembles, James often appeared shy in class or at chance encounters. This time, however, he approached me with animation: *Mr. A, you'll never guess. I got a FedEx package yesterday, with this sweatshirt!*

That's great! From Abbot Mark and Father Augustine?

Ya. He beamed and nodded; seeing James excited about college warmed my heart.

I think you'll be very happy at Saint Anselm. I certainly was.

He walked down the hall, laughing with his friends. Saint Anselm represented a new chapter and a new adventure for James, and I was happy for his growth. I had certainly continued to grow at Saint Anselm when I had graduated from Oakmont Regional some twenty years before.

When I returned home that afternoon, I also found a FedEx package at the door. The sender's address read 100 Saint Anselm Drive; inside I found a necktie with the college shield. *I guess they're proud of me, too.*

I made two trips to L.A. in May 2018, one for just twenty-four hours on May 12 and the other for a long weekend celebrating my sister's birthday the following weekend. Although *Faultlines* already had their listening party in April, they first performed their new album on May 12, right on Hollywood Boulevard. On arrival, I met John for lunch at a West Hollywood place called Granville.

Have you recovered from Peter Pan? he asked.

Onto my next project.

Do you know Evita is my favorite musical ever?

No, I didn't. You'll have to come. But that's not my next project.

What's your next project?

I'm buying a house in California.

The one in Palm Springs?

No, I wasn't crazy about Palm Springs. Where would you buy?

Joshua Tree. I love it there, and it's close to Palm Springs.

You've mentioned it.

What will you do with it when you're not there?

Rent it on Airbnb.

Joshua Tree is the right place for that.

Would you like to go in on this with me? Help me manage it.

Yes. I will, actually.

Are you serious?

Yeah. I have the time, I love it there. Let's make it work, friend.

I'm sure I looked gobsmacked. I expected he would say no, just as I had expected him to decline my invitation to London.

The following weekend Jenn and I took on California in a big way—it became my fifth trip since *Grease* and we drove out to Joshua Tree with John to look at houses. At Disneyland, Jenn and I wore our identical green "never grow up" t-shirts and raced to ride the Pirates of the Caribbean boats before standing in a nearly-endless line to ride "Peter Pan's Flight." The ship-shaped mechanical flying carts failed to rival Admiral Lantry's *Jolly Roger*, while the animatronic characters moved cutely but lacked the frustration of both of Oakmont's Peters, or the delightful conceit of Captain Hook, or the wit of Mr. Smee. Sure, Disney captured the familiar parts of the story, but, as I said to Jenn when we stepped back into the light, *we did it better than Walt.*

Ya, you did, she said. *But you really should have used my goats.*

Some day, Jenn. Some day I'll direct Doctor Dolittle and both of your goats can make their debut.

And the hedgehog?

Perhaps poking from the good Doctor's coat pocket, I teased.

Laughing, we again walked arm-in-arm as we had in London—only this time in the warmth of the California sun—toward King Arthur's Carousel.

"I taught you to fly. What more could there be?"
—J. M. Barrie, *Peter Pan and Wendy*

Encore

I'm really glad we met—Peter Pan and me. He, along with Kris and Dave, taught me about telling a good story—both the fairy tale and the story of our own adventure in Massachusetts—about believing in myself and in others, and about flying, imagining big ideas like pirate ships, and most especially, finding room for everyone who wanted to join our journey to Neverland. Like any good teacher, Peter Pan gave us all simple, memorable lessons with clear examples. Unlike Peter, however, we grew up as we learned to fly—all of us—becoming more imaginative, more daring, and more understanding. But again, ask yourself this: what would the world be like without Captain Hook? After all, he is just as memorable as the boy who wouldn't grow up.

I've never identified with Peter Pan, perhaps because I grew up too fast. I do, however, think I understand Captain Hook—not because I'm a menace, but I appreciate his complexity: refined, old world, melancholic, and sometimes a bit lonely. The Neverland story belongs not just to Peter or Hook, or maternal Wendy or worrying Mr. Darling, or brave Tiger Lily, or even Barrie or the Llewellyn Davies boys—it belongs to all of us, at least in the western imagination, and that, more than anything else, explains why the community responded so lovingly to the Oakmont production.

Close readers will notice that I used the past tense when referring not only to the 2018 production of *Peter Pan*, but to Oakmont generally. After the successful production of *Evita* in the spring of 2019, I took a medical leave of absence the following September, which I extended into a longer leave that became a permanent move to California, before I could reimagine *Doctor Dolittle* on stage. I love Oakmont and her students, but when I became acutely ill, I realized that my passion for all things Oakmont sometimes might have caused me more harm than good. At times, I felt neglected like the Lost Boys and Girls while at others I felt betrayed as if marooned by pirates. Certainly, I could have aimed for a better balance between work and home, but after a series of disappointments, frustrations, and changes, I let the wind blow me to a new community of artists. I navigated both push and pull factors—the strongest pull being a blossoming relationship that has given me new vitality and happiness. Kris has said repeatedly I've never sounded so happy. I do wish, however, my goodbye to both colleagues and students had been more deliberate, but the circumstances didn't allow for it despite my best efforts. Perhaps allow me this final valedictory, especially to the members of the Class of 2020: I gave Oakmont and Oakmont Theatre the best four years of my life, to the point of becoming sick, in teaching as well as producing *The Sound of Music, Grease, Evita,* and most especially, *Peter Pan.* We all grew together, but I think one student in particular grew most exceptionally: Victoria was a painfully-shy freshman when we met who blossomed on stage while confronting her personal challenges. While the entire Class of 2020 will always hold a fond place in my heart, Victoria in particular reminds me of the transformative power of theatre in the lives of young people and a community. *Brava* to her and her friends as they set out into the big world beyond Oakmont. I suppose if anything good can be found in my departure, at least I spared everyone from seeing my very teary goodbye. Except Kris.

In parting from Kris on the eve of Thanksgiving in 2019, in the basement garage of his Ashburnham home, we released our hug as I turned and walked into the dark night, feeling the cold rain mingle with the warm tears that streamed down my face. I choked on the misty air as I tried to catch my breath. Not a single day has passed when we've not texted each other from across the country, like when I asked him if he ever doubted if we could pull off the show.

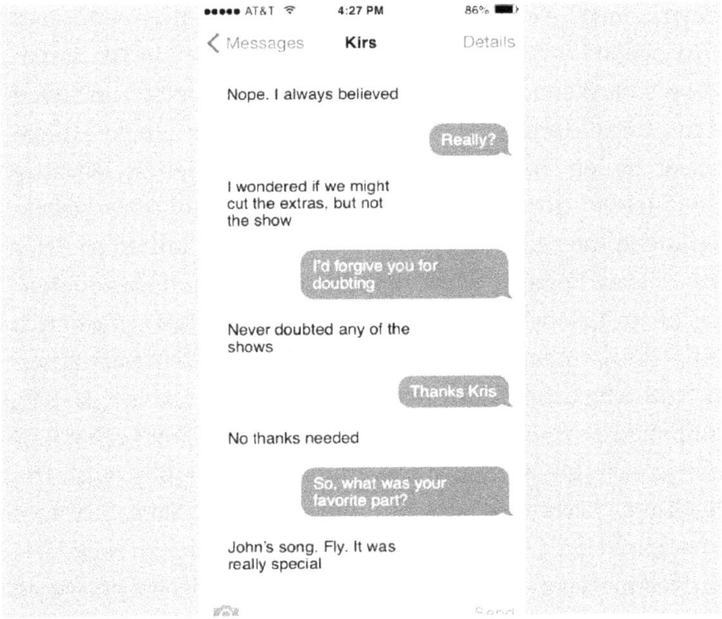

Sharon has become like a second mom to Kris. Her brilliance as a pianist is superseded only by her compassion and her dedication to teaching. Kris and Sharon have worked together longer than he's been a father. I imagine *Fly* was special for him, knowing what I had put into the show, into that specific moment, and the gift that I wanted to give to the kids that night with help from him, Sharon, and John. Now, as I sit and feel the long table boards in the Joshua Tree house, remembering that moment, I never would have known it was so special to Kris had I not asked.

The house in Joshua Tree that I own with John sits on an unfortunately-named street: Tonto Drive, near Walpi and not far from Apache and Cherokee. These names urge me to understand the challenges inherent in the Native American story beyond the classroom or stage. As reported in *The Boston Globe*, when Senator Warren learned that her ancestry included at most a sole ancestor some 640 generations ago, she made a clear apology to the leader of the Cherokee Nation, learning that ancestry does not equal tribal membership. The episode reminded me that these issues were hardly limited to *Peter Pan* or even Senator Warren; indeed, as I edited this book in July of 2019, Congresswoman Deb Haaland (D-NM), one of two indigenous women first elected to the House of Representatives in 2018 (the other, Congresswoman Sharice Davids, D-KS), published an opinion essay in *The New York Times* critical of an increasingly exclusive U.S. immigration policy, with the headline: "Trump Wants Immigrants to 'Go Back.' Native Americans Don't." She wrote, "If anyone can say 'go back,' it's Native Americans. My Pueblo ancestors, despite being targeted at every juncture—despite facing famine and drought—still inhabit this country today. But indigenous people aren't asking anyone to go back to where they came from." She emphasized the inclusive nature of the American promise noting that "those laying exclusive claim to the American dream lack a clear understanding of this country's history," and argued that indigenous cultures maintain a clear commitment to "lift up every community member so that no one is left behind," from the old to the young.

In defending an inclusive U.S. immigration policy, Congresswoman Haaland's words supported the ideas of the Humanities project at Oakmont: the genuine desire to hear from and include as many people as possible—all the while caring for youth and seniors. Native American culture is alive here in the Mojave alongside the neighboring Agua Caliente and Morongo Reservations and the Twenty-Nine Palms Band of Mission Indians. The Humanities work helped me grow as I learned to appreciate the world and its diverse people around me even more—both in Massachusetts and now in California.

Tonight after dinner, at our table with wide pine boards—not unlike those at Home Slice or The Swan in London—I asked my friend John a final question about *Peter Pan*.

I already told you everything! he groaned.

Here's my final question, I promise.

John sipped from his blue champagne flute—the same with which we toasted after *Fly*.

Describe the pirate ship in just one word, I said.

Big, he said with a gulp.

We laughed like Peter and the Lost Boys as we took our champagne and stepped out of our little house into the dark backyard. Together, we looked upwards toward—as Mr. Smee might say—the heights of the stars, the stars that led us all to Neverland.

Peter Pan

Oakmont Regional High School
April 26-28, 2018

Peter Pan……………….Amanda Porter
Peter's understudy…….Mary Mahoney
Wendy Darling……………..Mia Conte
John Darling………..Simon Rodriquenz
Michael Darling…………Kaden Aubin
Mr. Darling…………………..Max Carey
Mrs. Darling……………Mary Mahoney
Liza, the maid……………Emma Roche
Nana, the dog………Aiden Mawhinney
Jane……………………….Arianna Deery

Tiger Lily…………………..Eden Koljian

Braves of her Nation

Maddison Behringer
Phoebe Brooks
Lauren D'Attilio
Cayla DiAngelo
Gillian Dumas
Hannah Fells
Isabel Gelinas
Julia Kiedaisch
Maria Leger
Angela Lombardo
Thomas Paine
Leona Rameau
Sara Russo
Emily Watson

The Animals of Neverland

The Crocodile………..Stephen Altobelli
The Lion………………..Olivia Dubrule
The Monkey……………….Maria Brooks
The Kangaroo………….Alicyn Gormley
The Ostrich…………Abigail Wandless
The Giraffe………………Abigail Rusak
The Elephant…………….Anna Velardi

Captain Hook………….James Beaudry
Mr. Smee…………….Max Charbonneau
Starkey…………………..Cole Ellsworth
Cecco……………………Kalvin Richard
Noodler…………………..Oliver Wessels
Mullins…………………..Katelyn Murphy
Jukes……………………….Carson Stiles

The Crew of the Jolly Roger

William Babincsak
Mary Carpenter
Emmy Graham
Charlie Kovaleski
Sophia Koskinen
Ella Kreidler
Shannon Meehan
Eleanor Paine
Mackenzie Sullivan
Olivia Smith
Emma Tabor
Sage Valiton
Maddie Vassallo

The Lost Boys and Girls of Neverland

Slightly……………………..Alex Meehan
Curly……………………..Alyssa Varieur
Nibs………………………Madyson Aubin
Tootles…………………..James Maloney
1st Twin…………………..Tucker Rogers
2nd Twin…………………Cooper Rogers
Lost Boy…………………Victoria Leger
Lost Boy…………………Abigail Paradis
Lost Boy…………………..Ryan Maloney
Lost Boy…………………..Hiley Graham

Tinker Bell………………..Janelle Costa

IV

The End

At the end of the play, the director acknowledges very special people as well as gives notes to the even more special cast & crew.

Acknowledgment

Four people traveled with me on this journey more closely than anyone else; to Jenn, Kris, Dave, and John I give my heartfelt gratitude for flying to Neverland. I remain thankful for those families at Oakmont—especially the Aubin, Erickson, and Reitz families, Sharon Sawtell, and Karen Brown—who all adopted me like a Lost Boy. To my grandfather who, across many years nurtured my imagination by carving wooden swords like Peter's, as well as my parents who first taught me to hold a pencil: thank you. And to Ben, who didn't see *Peter Pan*, I'm so glad you're in the front row now, and in my neighborhood.

Bibliographic Essay

Although *Flight School* recounts the journey of the Ashburnham and Westminster communities on their 2018 flight to Neverland through my eyes, I drew heavily upon the experiences of others to understand the significance of this theatrical moment. Below, I have credited those with whom I corresponded and the sources I drew upon to write the story. Foremost, on the art of theatre direction generally, see **William Ball's** classic *A Sense of Direction* (Drama Book Pubs., 1984).

I am grateful to my colleagues, students, and neighbors for taking the time to write and share their Neverland experience with me by correspondence; namely, Dana Altobelli (May 22, 2019); Madyson Aubin (June 20, 2019); Keith Aubin (June 21, 2019); Bonnie Baer-Simahk (Oct. 3, 2017); Daniel Bartkus (Aug. 4, 2019); John Blackwell (Apr. 29, 2018); Lisa Brooks (Sept. 21, 2017); Karen Brown (May 20, 2019); Tammy Bucchino (Apr. 11, 2018); Timothy Caouette (May 20, 2019); Max Charbonneau (Apr. 26, 2018); Lauren D'Attilio (Apr. 11, 2018); Kris DeMoura (June 28, 2019); Dan Dufour (July 13, 2019 and May 20, 2019); Robert Goodby (Sept. 20, 2017); Cheryll Toney Holley (Sept. 20, 2017); Winifred Kender (July 26, 2019); Nicole Mahoney (Apr. 24, 2018); Gary Mazzola (June 13, 2019); Katelyn Murphy (June 29, 2019); Charles & Megan Reitz (Oct. 8, 2017); Emma Roche (July 15, 2019); Kara Roche (Apr. 3, 2018 and May 27, 2019); Abigail Rusak (June 18, 2019); Madeline Sayet (Sept. 19,

2017); Paula Stefanakos (July 11, 2019); Carson Stiles (June 17, 2019); as well as Christopher Wells (Apr. 17, 2017 and May 23, 2019) and Olivia Wells (July 21, 2019).

I drew some first-hand accounts from the *Peter Pan* playbill in 2018, including "How *Grease* Changed Me," by **Emma Reitz** and "Why I Take Part in Drama Club," by **Sara Russo**. Also in the *Peter Pan* playbill, both **Dr. Robert Goodby** and **Dr. James Stanley** provided scholar statements that explained the scope and value of the Oakmont Humanities project. In 2019, **Stephen Altobelli** wrote, "Why, as a Senior, I Became a Crocodile" for the *Evita* playbill, which recounted his personal experiences on stage like those of Emma and Sara in 2018. See also **Doneen Durling**, "Reinventing Peter Pan," in *The Gardner News* (April 17, 2018) for additional, local reporting.

Of course, the primary source for all things Peter Pan is **James Matthew Barrie's *Peter and Wendy***, published in the U.K. by Hodder & Stoughton and in the U.S. by Charles Scribner's Sons in 1911. The novel was published after the successful 1904 debut of *Peter Pan; or, the Boy Who Wouldn't Grow Up* at the Duke of York's Theatre, which later opened on Broadway in 1905. **92252 Press** has published a companion text to ***Flight School*** with the unabridged text and additional commentary. **Paramount Pictures** produced a silent version in 1924 before the story was adapted by the **Walt Disney Company** in 1953, just before the staging of **Jerome Robbins'** musical version starring Mary Martin in 1954 (now licensed by **Music Theatre International**). Several made-for-tv versions, as well as derivative films (such as ***Hook*** in 1991, ***Finding Neverland*** in 2004, NBC's 2014 ***Peter Pan Live!*** and contemporary with this publication, a new film by Benh Zeitlin entitled ***Wendy*** in 2020) and marionette productions like that of Mabou Mines, have kept the Neverland story firmly in the public consciousness for a century. The Walt Disney Company is producing a live action version of their 1953 animated feature beginning in 2020, with no release date yet set.

This project relied upon the 1904 script and 1911 novel—both by Barrie—as well as the 1954 Broadway script (which is the version Oakmont produced in 2018). While theatre critic **Brooks Atkinson** reviewed *Peter Pan* for *The New York Times* with much praise but also included some criticism in his article: "The transformation of Peter Pan into an American musical show is not all beer and skittles. Most of the music and lyrics are on a lower level than Barrie; most of the songs rob Peter Pan of literary distinction....the music as a whole is insensitive to improvisation." See his "Peter Pan: Mary Martin Plays in an Americanized version of Barrie's Fairy Story," (October 31, 1954, X1) for more.

The website of the **Great Ormond Street Hospital for Children** includes important information about the relationship between the institution and Barrie (see www.gosh.org/about-us/peter-pan). Other biographical and contextual information about Barrie was gleaned from **Norman Allen**, "Peter Pan Turns 100" in *Smithsonian Magazine* (Dec. 2004) and **Andrew Birken**, *J. M. Barrie & the Lost Boys* (Yale U.P., 2003).

There is no shortage of literary criticism surrounding Peter or the other characters. Works by folklorist **Jack Zipes** are always a helpful starting point in examining the ways these stories shape culture and society and it's worth reading his Introduction to the 2004 Penguin edition of *Peter Pan* as well as his "Negating History and Male Fantasies through Psychoanalytic Criticism" in *Children's Literature* (vol. 18, 1990). Both **Tracy Davis** and **Ann Wilson** examined the changing class structure predicated by the Industrial Revolution and the manifestation this impact had on *Peter Pan*. They both discuss Tinker Bell, who was so-named because she "mends fairy pots and kettles," and implies a working-class even among fairies "in ways that are consistent with the middle class's imagining of the working class" (Wilson 605). Davis links the name "Tinker" with the Scottish name for gypsies who also represented a "childlike, playful, [and] a people who never grow up" (Davis 68). For more, see Davis, "Do You Believe in Fairies?" in *Theatre Journal* (no. 57, 2005) and Wilson, "Hauntings: Anxiety, Technology, and Gender in *Peter Pan*," in *Modern Drama* (no. 43.4, 2000).

The work of the Humanities project, funded by Mass Humanities, was driven by the **Code of Ethics Related to Native Americans from the National Endowment for the Humanities**, available at www.neh.gov/grants/manage/code-ethics-related-native-americans and proved foundational in the ways the committee both thought about and approached the work—including issues of vocabulary. In an attempt to better understand the issues surrounding Native American representation, in particular, President Trump's pejorative use of the heroine Pocahontas' name, I read **Camilla Townsend's** *Pocahontas and the Powhatan Dilemma* (Farrar, Straus and Giroux, 2005) and **Jackie Mansky's** "The True Story of Pocahontas," in *Smithsonian Magazine* (March 23, 2017). Both provided helpful context for understanding **Jess Bidgood's** "Elizabeth Warren faces new questions about heritage amid apology effort," in *The Boston Globe* (February 5, 2019). Looking even closer to home at the Amherst controversy, **Scott Merzbach's** "Area man wants Amherst to change town's name" in the *Greenfield Recorder* (August 21, 2017) and **George Graham's** "Will Lord Jeffrey Amherst controversy lead to additional name changes in town that commemorates Indigenous Peoples' Day?" on *MassLive.com* (Oct 8, 2018) proved particularly helpful. Citing a letter written by Cullen Murphy, former chair of the Amherst College Board of Trustees, Graham points out that the name of the College was drawn from the town itself—not the general. **Daniella Zalcman**, who first contacted me by email on Apr. 18, 2018) published her piece on Native American representation with Mark Trahant in the December 2019 issue of *National Geographic Magazine* as "Native American Imagery is All Around Us, While the People Are Often," without mention of Oakmont. In the same issue, **Tristan Ahtone's** "Reclaiming Our Stories" featured an interview with **Madeline Sayet** (madelinesayet.com), who wrote to me on Sept. 20, 2017.

An important, contemporary (July 22, 2019) op-ed in *The New York Times* by Native American Congresswoman **Deb Haaland** of New Mexico, "Trump Wants Immigrants to 'Go Back.' Native Americans Don't," provides both a short-term critique of Trump's immigration policy alongside a longer-term perspective of indigenous history in North America, which is important to the ongoing discussion of the president's derogatory use of the name "Pocahontas" for Senator Warren. Lastly, my own graduate work in the field of ethnographic history offers an introductory background to the problem generally and a more extensive bibliography of contemporary and colonial sources than what is given here. See my *Dichotomous Utilitarian Discourse of the Amerindian: A Consequence of Policy, Ethnography, and Intellect in the Colonial Atlantic World* (2004) available from the Amelia V. Gallucci-Cirio Library and Archives at Fitchburg State University as well as in my essay "Indian Wars" in **Bill Marshall's** encyclopedia *France and the*

Americas: Culture, Politics, and History (ABC-Clio, 2005).

The composition of this book coincided with a 2019 renaissance of interest in, and love for, **Mr. Fred Rogers**, first in the documentary "Won't You Be My Neighbor" by filmmaker Morgan Neville and then in Marielle Heller's feature film "A Beautiful Day in the Neighborhood" starring Tom Hanks. During the editing phase of the book, I traveled to the **Fred Rogers Center at Saint Vincent College in Latrobe, PA** to understand more about Mr. Rogers' unique way of imagining and storytelling. I now find myself constantly finding quotes from Mr. Rogers, especially from the "@MisterRogersSay" feed on *Twitter* as well as in books like *Life's Journeys According to Mister Rogers* (Hatchett Books 2005). Mr. Rogers' articulation of values such as respect, inclusion, and especially imagination guided Kris and I's work in producing *Peter Pan* in 2018 (perhaps drawn from our subconscious of watching Mr. Rogers on public television in the 1980s) but also in my introduction to the special children's performance where I mentioned "Mr. Rogers & the Wicked Witch of the West, Margaret Hamilton (1975)" available on *YouTube.* I was pleased to see a picture of Mr. Rogers and Mrs. Hamilton on display in the Rogers Center—not all that far from the Daniel Tiger.

Finally, a good part of this story is about the creation of a new chapter—or better yet, verse—to the Peter Pan story, that of **John Flanagan's *Fly*.** I commissioned John to write it, on the condition that he perform the song himself, for the cast and crew of Oakmont's 2018 production. The photograph of that performance, along with the photograph of the DeMoura family, was taken by Sue O'Connor. The beautiful lyrics and sweet melody of *Fly* belong to John, and you can see the performance for yourself at my website: **jeffreywaubuchon.com**.

Notes

ACT I, SCENE 1: KRIS

1 Oakmont Regional High School has staged the following musicals in the last thirty years, ranging from the classic to the contemporary: *The Sound of Music* (1988), *Brigadoon* (1989), The *Pajama Game* (1991), *Oklahoma!* (1992), *Fiddler on the Roof* (1993), *Once Upon a Mattress* (1996), *Cinderella* (1997), *Grease* (1999), *Once on This Island* (2000), *Damn Yankees* (2002), *Guys & Dolls* (2004), *Kiss Me Kate* (2005), *Bye, Bye Birdie* (2006), *Hello, Dolly!* (2007), *Anything Goes* (2008), *The Music Man* (2009), *Into the Woods* (2010), *Les Misérables* (2011), *Urinetown* (2012), *Young Frankenstein* (2013), *Thoroughly Modern Millie* (2014), *Seussical* (2015), *The Sound of Music* (2016), *Grease* (2017), *Peter Pan* (2018), and *Evita* (2019). The 2020 production was cancelled because of the coronavirus pandemic.

2 Data from the 2010 Census (census.gov) and Zillow.com (July 22, 2019). While household incomes in both towns sit above average, median home values are below the state average. In Ashburnham, the median home value is $266,347 and again, just slightly higher in Westminster at $270,456—but compare those to the state median of $409,600.

3 I am grateful to Oakmont E.S.L. teacher Barbara Cohen for these insights.

4 Kris calls the 2002 production of *Damn Yankees* "the show of three directors" as it was tossed between then-English teachers Mark Santos and Betty Lilly, with Kris serving as music director before Sandy was hired.

5 In chapter 3, Barrie notes that only lost boys live in Neverland because girls "are much too clever to fall out of their prams" and fly away. I maintain fidelity to Barrie's idea of the Lost Boys, but I augment the group by writing (and Girls) because, of course in 2018, we see girls on Neverland—as did Behn Zeitland in his 2020 film *Wendy*.

ACT I, SCENE 4: DAVE

6 My parents, Paul and Debbie, also contributed to the financial success of Peter Pan by donating fresh-baked cookies and other items from their

store in Harmonyville, Vermont. As I wrote in the playbill to thank them, they have been supporting educational programs in the Ashburnham-Westminster Regional School District since 1985.

ACT I, SCENE 5: JEFF

7 Specifically, their website reads: Mass Humanities rarely funds "theatrical and artistic productions—unless the performers and production personnel (actors, stage hands, scriptwriters, etc.) are a primary audience benefiting from the project's humanities content." See "What We Fund," masshumanities.org.

8 Andrew Birken, *J. M. Barrie & the Lost Boys* (Yale University Press, 2003).

ACT I, SCENE 6: KRIS

9 The Wampanoag story did not fade into the myth of children's storybooks but intersects with the ongoing pejorative use of the Pocahontas slur preferred by President Trump. The Wampanoags made headlines in March of 2020, in the midst of the first coronavirus outbreak in the United States, when Interior Secretary David Bernhardt announced that, as a result of a recent case heard by a three-judge panel of the First Circuit Court of Appeals—which included former Supreme Court Justice David Souter—the Department of the Interior had no authority to hold land in trust for the Mashpee Wampanoags because the tribe was only recognized by the US government in 2007 and not by the Indian Reorganization Act of 1934. The court, however, ordered nothing to be done, only instead articulated that the Department lacked the authority to hold land in trust. Legislation drafted by Rep. Bill Keating of Massachusetts to solidify recognition of the trust was harshly decried by President Trump in a tweet on May 8, 2019: "Republicans shouldn't vote for H.R. 312, a special interest casino Bill [sic], backed by Elizabeth (Pocahontas) Warren. It is unfair and doesn't treat Native Americans equally." The bill, however, eventually passed in the House of Representatives 275 to 146 roughly along party lines, although it has not yet been taken up in the Senate. The subsequent decision to release the Wampanoags' land without a court order suggests that reservation lands across the United States could be taken out of trust at the discretion of the Department. As headlines decried the loss of recognized tribal status, the Department stressed that the *"Mashpee Wampanoag Tribe remains a federally recognized Tribe"* while Cedric Cromwell, Chairman of the Wampanoag Tribe, called for the maintenance of this recognition: "We have survived, we will continue to survive," he wrote. "These are our

lands, these are the lands of our ancestors, and these will be the lands of our grandchildren. This Administration has come and it will go. But we will be here, always. And we will not rest until we are treated equally with other federally recognized tribes and the status of our reservation is confirmed." See Cedric Cromwell, *We Will Take Action to Prevent the Loss of Our Land,* 28 March 2020 at mashpeewampanoagtribe-nsn.gov; the Department of the Interior, *Press Statement Regarding the Court Decision Requiring Interior to Take the Mashpee Wampanoag Tribe's Land Out of Trust,* 30 March 2020, at doi.gov; *and,* WBUR News, *Secretary Of Interior Orders Mashpee Wampanoag Reservation 'Disestablished,' Tribe Says*, 28 March 2020, at wbur.org.

10 See the *Smithsonian Magazine* article, "The True Story of Pocahontas," by Jackie Mansky (March 23, 2017) at smithsonianmag.com.

ACT II, SCENE 5: DAVE

11 By way of comparison to Broadway, in 2017 the *CATS* Playbill at the Neil Simon Theatre ran sixty-four pages and the Palace Theatre's Playbill for *Sunset Boulevard,* with Glenn Close stealing the glossy cover as Norma Desmond, filled a mere fifty-two pages.

ACT III, SCENE 2: KRIS

12 Each year I point out the fact that three of the four music teachers in the Ashburnham and Westminster schools—Kris DeMoura, Joe Lordan, and Kris Lucander—also play as professional musicians in the orchestra. The musical ability of our students, and the quality of Kris's orchestra, is due so much to the combined efforts of these educators along with Mindy Lordan who is the music teacher in Ashburnham. Kris Lucander also played Captain von Trapp in the 1988 Oakmont production of *The Sound of Music.*

ACT III, SCENE 3: JOHN & KRIS

13 At the Saturday night show I auctioned a whimsical painting of Neverland created and donated by a dedicated stage mom and artist, Laurie Tarr Ellsworth (see her portfolio at https://www.lte-studio.com/). The painting fetched more than $500 and was bought by the parents of a member of the junior class. When I brought them the painting at the end of the performance, they refused to take it. Instead, they gave it to me as a memento of our collective flight with Peter Pan. It's a treasure and it hangs in my Joshua Tree office, reminding me of the generosity of so many families that helped on that journey.

About the Author

Jeffrey William Aubuchon returned to Oakmont Regional High School in 2011, thirteen years after graduating. Beyond directing theatre and teaching history there, he advised the student group apush4peace that has raised thousands of dollars for Peace Corps projects worldwide. Now he writes and coaches other writers among California's Joshua trees. He studied in the liberal arts tradition with the Benedictine monks and faculty of Saint Anselm College, where he graduated *magna cum laude*, and later earned a master's degree from the creative writing faculty at Harvard University. Follow him on Twitter @JeffreyAubuchon and subscribe to his blog at jeffreywaubuchon.com.

Also by Jeffrey W. Aubuchon

Both titles are published by 92252 Press and sold on Amazon.com as well as with independent booksellers like IndieBound.org. Available NOW!

The Companion to Peter and Wendy
"All children, except one, grow up." So begins Sir James M. Barrie's classic story of *Peter and Wendy* and their flight to Neverland. Here is the original 1911 Peter Pan novel, reprinted in its entirety with a new introduction and commentary by writer and stage director Jeffrey Aubuchon. $1 from every book sold is donated to Great Ormond Street Hospital for Children in London.

Three Desert Stories
The Sahara is home to the indigenous Berbers and their camels, making this wilderness as much a sanctuary of the human spirit as a wasteland. These three short stories relate the young American Dylan's vivid and dramatic journey across the Moroccan desert before sharing the legend of a Berber girl, Maryam, whom he encounters. $1 from every book sold goes to the Peace Corps Partnership Program to extend the global promise of U.S. friendship.

Lightning Source UK Ltd.
Milton Keynes UK
UKHW020700270520
363938UK00011B/449

9 781734 059236